Round Hall Nutshells

TORT
(Second Edition)

Round Hall Nutshells

TORT
(Second Edition)

URSULA CONNOLLY

ROUND HALL   THOMSON REUTERS

Published in 2009 by
Thomson Reuters (Professional) Ireland Limited
(Registered in Ireland, Company No. 80867.
Registered Office and address for service
43 Fitzwilliam Place, Dublin 2)
trading as Round Hall

Typeset by
Carrigboy Typesetting Services

Printed by
Colour Books, Dublin

ISBN 978–1–85800–538–6

A catalogue record for this book
is available from the British Library.

Views expressed by each author are the views of that author alone and do
not necessarily represent the views of other authors or the editors.

PREFACE

This book is intended to provide an introduction to the principles of tort law and an overview of the primary torts in a manner which is as comprehensive as possible without befuddling the reader. To aid in the understanding of the torts discussed the facts of a number of cases are given. This is not intended to replace the reading of the cases themselves, but more to help in understanding the torts in a factual context. As such this text provides an excellent basis for further study of the law of torts and a helpful guide for the purposes of revising the fundamental principles.

As with the first edition, care has been taken in this second edition to include significant recent developments. Important recent cases, such as *Fitzpatrick v White* [2007] I.E.S.C. 51 on informed consent (Chapter 10), and *McGrath v Trintech Technologies Ltd* [2005] 4 I.R. 382 and *Berber v Dunnes Stores* [2009] I.E.S.C. 10 on liability for mental injury (Chapter 8) are included. Recent reform and proposals for reform are also discussed. In particular, the provisions of the Defamation Act 2009, which has brought about a significant reform of the tort of defamation, are discussed.

The author would like to thank Gabi Honan, Law Librarian, NUI Galway, for her research assistance and the staff at Round Hall for their work in the publication of this book. All responsibility for errors and omissions rests with the author.

URSULA CONNOLLY

TABLE OF CONTENTS

TABLE OF CASES

IRISH CASES

OTHER CASES

TABLE OF LEGISLATION

CONSTITUTIONAL PROVISIONS

IRISH STATUTES

OTHER IRISH LEGISLATION

EUROPEAN LEGISLATION

1. NATURE AND FUNCTION OF
THE LAW OF TORTS

INTRODUCTION

The area of tort law covers a wide range of wrongs committed by one person against another. It deals with situations as diverse as slippages in supermarkets and pubs, to car accidents, bus collisions, the viewing of a traumatic event, assault, defamation, defective products and the giving of negligent advice. The range of injury it seeks to compensate is equally diverse, ranging from physical injuries, psychological injuries and in some cases economic injury. It is this dynamism that makes it a hugely interesting subject to study but also a difficult one to define or classify into neat categories. We will see that given the dynamic nature of jurisprudence in this area some torts are of recent origin while other more traditional torts are in a constant state of development. This book seeks to act as an aid in the study of tort law by providing an introduction to the fundamental principles and an analysis of some of the major torts.

Firstly however, it is important to examine the nature of tort law and establish where it lies in relation to the other major branches of the law. The word "tort" is derived from the Medieval Latin word *tortum*, and means a civil wrong, i.e. a wrong committed between private parties. It covers those wrongs that arise because of a breach of a duty imposed by law, as opposed to duties imposed by contract. The wrong may have occurred because of an intentional act (such as trespass) but in the vast majority of cases the area of tort law deals with the commission of unintentional harm or injury.

The remedy sought is generally compensation in the form of monetary damages although in some cases an injunction may be a more appropriate remedy. In the case where damages are awarded the guiding principle of the court is to place the victim in the position he or she would have been in had the tort not arisen. While this is often an impossible task (how does one compensate the loss of an arm for instance?) the courts have established guidelines on the matter. Legislation also plays an important role in the division of liability and the assessment of damages (see further Chapters 16 and 17).

ACTIONS IN TORT

An action in tort is a civil action, i.e. an action between private parties. It thus forms part of the civil law. The person who carries out the tort is termed a "tortfeasor" and when being sued is referred to as the defendant, while the victim is the claimant or plaintiff. The court in which a claimant brings an action depends on the level of compensation which is sought, subject to the maximum limits of each of those courts.

The basis for liability differs depending on the tort in question. In the tort of negligence for instance a duty of care must exist and there must be a clear breach of this duty. For other torts, such as the strict liability tort of nuisance, liability hinges on the unreasonableness of the behaviour in question. In others still, such as defamation, what it required is that the statement made is one which is capable of being defamatory. In all torts the defendant must have caused the act or the injury (causation) and the type of damage caused must be foreseeable (remoteness) except in cases where no damage is required (torts which are actionable per se). The absence or otherwise of an appropriate defence must also be explored before a breach can be compensated.

Since May 31, 2004 all personal injury claims relating to employers' liability, motor liability and public liability must first be presented to a body established by the State to deal with personal injuries cases, called the InjuriesBoard.ie (formerly known as the Personal Injuries Assessment Board). This body, established by statute (the Personal Injuries Assessment Board Act 2003), deals with cases where fault is not contested. Compensation is calculated based on written evidence submitted by the claimant (including a medical report of injuries suffered) and by reference to amounts set out in the Book of Quantum (this Book is publicly available, please see *www.injuriesboard.ie*). If the claim is contested, or if either party is unhappy with the award, then the claim can be released to be dealt with by the courts.

TORTIOUS LIABILITY AND OTHER BRANCHES OF THE LAW

The wrongs which are capable of constituting an action in tort can also give rise to an action in other areas of the law. A breach by an employer of his duty to provide a safe place of work for instance is also a breach of contract, as all employment contracts contain an implied term of a right to a safe place of work. This section will examine the interaction between tort law and other branches of the law.

Tort Law and the Constitution

The fundamental document enshrining all of our basic rights as citizens is the 1937 Constitution (Bunreacht na hÉireann). Constitutional rights consist of both enumerated rights: that is to say those that are explicitly stated, such as the right to property and the right to education; and unenumerated rights, that is to say those which have been developed by the courts on the basis of a stated Constitutional provision. Some rights protected by the law of torts will invariably overlap with those protected by the Constitution.

The guiding principle in relation to the balance to be struck between constitutional law and tort law can be found in the case of *Hanrahan v Merck Sharpe & Dohme (Ireland) Ltd* [1988] I.L.R.M. 629. It established that recourse to the Constitution should not be had where that right is effectively protected by another branch of the law. As stated by Henchy J., once a plaintiff "... founds his action on an existing tort he is normally confined to the limitations of that tort ... [unless] ... it could be shown that the tort in question is basically ineffective to protect his constitutional rights".

This finding has also found support in the case of *W v Ireland (No. 2)* [1997] 2 I.R.141. Here Costello J. stated that there were two types of rights within the Constitution:

- The first which were protected by law, either by statute or in tort. In such instances the courts would not impose a remedy under the Constitution, unless it could be established that existing remedies were ineffective (see also Barrington J. in *Meskell v CIE* [1971] I.R. 121 who delivered a similar judgment). However, if a breach in tort is also a breach of a Constitutional right it may be a reason to grant exemplary damages.
- The second, which were not protected by laws outside of the Constitution, and would result in a remedy of damages for breach of a Constitutional right.

Tort and European Law

A few words on the source of European rights might be useful before we begin our discussion of what McMahon & Binchy have termed "euro-torts". Sources of European rights include Treaty articles, Directives, and regulations. It is in the area of Directives that we are primarily concerned. While Directives are drafted and implemented on a European level, individuals cannot rely on them until one of the following occurs: the Member State implements the Directive in the form of an Act or other instrument in the Member State, or alternatively where the date for doing so has elapsed. In some instances, the Member State fails to implement the directive on time, leading to a loss on the part of an individual. In *Francovich and Bonifaci v Italy* [1991] ECR I–5357, the European Court of Justice held that a Member State was obliged to pay compensation for any damages arising from such a failure.

In terms of identifying a breach and its link to the damage caused, the process is very similar to that which occurs in the tort of negligence. There must be damage brought about by the breach of the State's duty to implement a law. In the case of *Tate v Minister for Social Welfare* [1995] 1 I.L.R.M. 507, Carroll J. held that "there is nothing strange in describing the States failure to fulfill its obligations under the Treaty as a tort."

Tort and the Criminal Law

Unlike the situation that arises under constitutional law, an action can be pursued under both criminal and tort law for the same wrong or offence, albeit in entirely different ways. Not only will the nature of the action be very different but the resulting remedy will also fulfill an entirely different function. Crimes are generally seen as offences against the public at large, e.g. murder, dangerous driving or malicious injury to property. As such they are the subject of prosecution by the State following which if the defendant is found guilty the punishment will be imprisonment or a fine payable to the State. While the criminal law may provide for compensation to be paid to the victim under recent initiatives introduced by legislation such as the Criminal Justice Act 1993, this is not fundamentally the purpose of criminal law. On the other hand, offences that are crimes can also be the subject of tort actions. For example an incident of assault can give rise to a criminal prosecution by the State and also a claim for damages by the victim of the assault. The purpose of the remedy in tort is not fundamentally to punish but rather to provide compensation to the victim in the form of damages, or as stated earlier, an injunction.

Tort and Contract Law

Despite the fact that contract and tort both occupy the realm of private law, there are still significant differences between the two. An action in contract is only possible when you enjoy privity of contract, i.e. where you are a party to the contract. No such requirement exists in tort. The terms of a contract are those agreed by the parties while the principles of tort are those established by the courts. There are also differences in burdens of proof, limitation periods and the position regarding damages (tort seeks to compensate for injury suffered whereas contract is largely concerned with compensation for loss of future expectations). The right to be heard by a jury in tort but not in contract cases had also existed prior to the Courts Act 1988 but this is no longer the case, with the exception of defamation cases in the High Court and actions for intentional trespass to the person.

Where a plaintiff has an action in both contract and tort they may take the action under both. In the case of *Finlay v Murtagh* [1979] I.R. 249 the claimant who sought to bring a professional negligence action in tort against the defendant solicitor was not debarred from doing so simply because a contract existed.

A contract may however override the duty in tort where such a provision is clearly stated in the contract. So where for instance a contract states that no liability will arise in a particular instance or where the contract clearly excludes the right to bring an action, the courts will not override this provision if it is deemed to have been a clear term of the contract. As stated by O'Flaherty J. in *Pat O'Donnell & Co Ltd v Truck & Machinery Sales Ltd* [1998] 4 I.R. 197 at 200:

"… the general duty in tort cannot be manipulated so as to override the contractual allocation of responsibility between the parties. Thus if, for instance, a contract provides, whether expressly or by necessary implication, that the defendant is not liable for a particular risk, then the law of tort should not be allowed to contradict it."

2. CAUSATION AND REMOTENESS

INTRODUCTION

To receive a remedy in tort the plaintiff must show that the defendant caused the injury or loss complained of (causation) and that the resulting injury is not one so far removed from the act of the defendant that he cannot be held liable for it (remoteness). Causation is an essential element of all torts for which injury is a necessary element (i.e. for torts which are not actionable per se).

In deciding the question of causation the plaintiff must prove that the defendant was both the factual cause (*causa sine qua non*) and the legal cause (*causa causans*) of the injury. Factual causation considers whether the defendant caused in a factual sense the injury complained of, and is decided both on the basis of a common sense approach and by the application of a number of tests (most typically the "but for" test and the "material contribution test"). Establishing factual causation is not determinative of liability however, and the plaintiff is required to further prove that the defendant was a legal cause of the injury suffered. Legal causation considers whether there is an intervening act, a *novus actus interveniens*, which will break the chain of causation and free the defendant from liability. The standard applied is generally that of the balance of probabilities, but a relaxation of this standard is applied in certain cases (see Material Contribution below). Finally, the plaintiff must prove that the injury suffered is not too remote from the defendant's act to attract compensation (the question of remoteness). This final examination is considered part of legal causation by some commentators.

This chapter will discuss who must prove causation, the tests for establishing factual and legal causation and the principles applied when considering remoteness of damage.

WHO MUST PROVE CAUSATION?

It is for the plaintiff to demonstrate, generally on the balance of probabilities, that the defendant caused the damage. Despite the potential evidential hardship of this rule from the plaintiff's perspective, the courts have consistently held that the burden ought not be reversed.

This view was affirmed by Murphy J. in the case of *Cosgrave v Ryan and the Electricity Supply Board* [2003] 1 I.L.R.M. 544, where he stated "Causation must be proved by the plaintiff. Any argument in relation to the shifting of the onus of proof in respect of breach of duty of care cannot extend to the fundamental issue of causation" and more recently in *Quinn v Mid Western Health Board* [2005] I.E.S.C. 19 where Kearns J. said:

> "Any approach which had the effect of reversing the onus of proof, or transferring the onus of proof to the defendant, would be one of such importance, even in the few exceptional cases where it might be appropriate, that it would require a full court—or perhaps even legislation—before a change of such magnitude to existing law could take place."

DETERMINING THE FACTUAL CAUSE(S)

Determination of the factual cause(s) involves a factual or scientific examination of the defendant's actions to see if they can be held to have caused the plaintiff's injury. The courts for this purpose have developed two principal tests, the "but for" test and the "material contribution" test. This stage is said to act as a preliminary filter, after which a determination of the legal cause takes place.

"But for" Test

The most commonly used test used to apportion responsibility is the "but for" test, sometimes referred to as the "what if" test. What is asked is, "But for the action of the defendant would the injury have arisen?" If the answer is in the negative then the defendant can be included as one of the factual causes. If on the other hand the injury would have arisen regardless of the actions of the defendant, notwithstanding any negligence on his or her part, the defendant will not be held to be a factual cause.

One of the leading cases which applied this test was the case of *Barnett v Chelsea and Kensington Hospital Management Committee* [1969] 1 Q.B. 428. In this case the plaintiff's husband, a night watchman, suffered from severe abdominal pains and attended a hospital following his night shift. He was one of three people turned away from the hospital without having been given a proper examination by a doctor. He subsequently died of arsenic poisoning and his wife sued the hospital for negligence. It was clear that the hospital had not carried out a proper examination of the plaintiff's spouse, but was this a cause of the spouse's death? The court in applying the "but for" test held that he would have died anyway given the nature of the poisoning. Despite the negligence of the hospital it was not the effective cause of the injury and the hospital was not held liable.

The "but for" test is useful in cases where there is only one defendant but can throw up peculiar results where there is more than one concurrent cause of an injury. Take for instance the case where in a car accident two cars collide with the claimant's car causing damage. Using the "but for" test both would escape liability, as the injury would have occurred regardless of any one defendant's actions. To address this anomaly the "material contribution test" may be used.

Material Contribution Test

This test states that a defendant's act is said to be a causative factor if it materially contributed to the plaintiff's injury (see *Bonnington Castings Ltd v Wardlaw* [1956] A.C. 613 where an employer was found liable for an employee's injury from inhaling silica dust as it was probable that the negligent exposure was a "material contribution" to the injury suffered). The "material contribution" test can also find a defendant liable where conduct which is not tortious in itself, may be so when taken together with the conduct of others. This arose in the case of *Lambton v Mellish* [1894] 3 Ch 163. In this case two fairground workers (Mellish and Cox) operated merry-go-rounds that were accompanied by organs. The plaintiff, who lived nearby, sued in nuisance. It was argued by the defendants that as each defendant taken alone did not constitute a nuisance, neither of them was liable. The court rejected this finding, stating that both parties will be liable if their actions taking together cause harm, regardless of whether the actions of any one taken alone would constitute a tort, as each had made a material contribution to the nuisance.

In the English case of *Fairchild v Glenhaven Funeral Services* [2002] 3 All E.R. 305 a more generous test was applied allowing for causation to be established where the defendant's act "materially increased the *risk*" of the injury arising. The House of Lords held that the rule would apply where the defendant's act was tortious and capable of giving rise to the injury but where scientific evidence could not establish if the defendant was responsible. In *Fairchild* the plaintiff had contracted mesothelioma, a disease which can be triggered by exposure to one fibre of asbestos. As the plaintiff had been exposed by different employers to asbestos at different times it was impossible to say which had caused his illness. The House of Lords found that all could be held liable as they had all "materially increased the risk" of Fairchild developing mesothelioma.

DETERMINING THE LEGAL CAUSE: *NOVUS ACTUS INTERVENIENS*

A *novus actus interveniens*, or new intervening act, is capable of breaking the chain of causation and relieving the initial defendant of liability. The intervening act may be that of a third party, of the plaintiff himself or it may be an independent cause, such as an act of God. While not all intervening acts will amount to a *novus actus* the rules for distinguishing a *novus actus* from an otherwise innocent intervening act are less than clear. Some general principles have emerged, focusing on issues of the foreseeability and reasonableness of the intervening act, and to a lesser extent the criminal nature of it.

Foreseeability

In general, the more foreseeable the intervening act the more unlikely it will be that the courts will deem it a *novus actus*. A number of cases are illustrative of this principle. In the case of *Crowley v AIB and O'Flynn* [1988] I.L.R.M. 225 the plaintiff was injured when he fell off the flat roof of the premises owned by AIB. The architects who designed the roof escaped liability on the basis that AIB allowing the boys to play there was unforeseeable, thereby constituting a *novus actus* which broke the chain of causation. The issue of the foreseeability of the plaintiff's actions and whether they could constitute a *novus actus* has also arisen in a number of cases. It appears that if the behaviour of the plaintiff is the "natural and probable" (i.e. foreseeable) consequence of the defendant's actions then it will not be deemed to constitute a *novus actus*. In the English case of *Wieland v Cyril Lord Carpets* [1969] 3 All E.R. 1006 for instance the plaintiff's actions in descending a stairway in her home were found to be reasonable and did not constitute a *novus actus*. She had been unable to use her bifocals (spectacles) because of a neck injury caused by the defendant's actions. However, if the plaintiff acts unreasonably then the defendant will not be held liable for any further injury caused (*McKew v Holland* [1969] 2 All E.R. 1621).

In terms of when a criminal intervening act can constitute a *novus actus* again the real question is whether that act is foreseeable. A criminal intervening act may absolve the defendant of liability (*Lamb v Camden LBC* [1981] Q.B.) but not where the criminal act is the very thing the defendant ought to have guarded against or foreseen (*Stansbie v Troman* [1948] 2 K.B. 48). The more recent decision (affirmed in the Supreme Court) of *Breslin v Corcoran and the Motor Insurers Bureau of Ireland* [2003] 2 I.L.R.M. 189 returned to the question of whether an intervening criminal act is foreseeable. In this case the first defendant, Corcoran, left his car unattended with the keys in the ignition while he went to get a sandwich. Predictably the car was stolen and the thief, when driving away at high speed, injured the plaintiff, Breslin. In this case the court made a distinction between the act of stealing the car and the act of reckless driving. The first the court held was foreseeable. However the second, that of reckless driving, was not. As it was this act which had caused the injury the reckless driving constituted a *novus actus* to relieve the first named defendant of liability. As stated by Fennelly J.:

> "It is ... necessary to ask whether it was probable that the unattended car, if taken, would be driven so carelessly as to cause damage to others. In my view, there is nothing in the present case to suggest that the first-named defendant should have anticipated as a reasonable probability that the car, if stolen, would be driven so carelessly as to cause injury to another user of the road such as the plaintiff."

Recklessness

In the case where the intervening act is either unreasonable or reckless, then it may well constitute a *novus actus*. The standard is a subjective as opposed to an objective one, i.e. did the person avert to the possibility of the risk but nonetheless act in reckless disregard of it. In *Conole v Redbank Oyster Co* [1976] I.R. 191, the recklessness of a captain in taking a boat out to sea which he knew to be unseaworthy, was found to constitute a *novus actus* relieving the otherwise culpable manufacturers of liability.

DIVISION OF LIABILITY IN CASES WHERE MULTIPLE CAUSES EXIST

Where a number of parties cause *different damage* each must be sued separately for the damage caused. Where a number of parties, together or separately, simultaneously or successively, cause the *same damage*, they are referred to as concurrent wrongdoers (s.11 of the Liability Act 1961) and may be held jointly liable (in which case each defendant is liable for all the injury) or severally liable (in which case each defendant is only responsible for that part of the injury caused). In *Performance Cars Ltd v Abraham* [1961] 3 All E.R. 413 for instance, the defendant was found not be responsible for the respraying of a car he had collided with as this damage had already been caused by an earlier collision. In Ireland, division of liability between concurrent wrongdoers is dealt with by Pt III of the Civil Liability Act 1961. Section 11(3) of the Civil Liability Act 1961 deals with situations where it is unclear which party caused the injury and states that:

> "Where two or more persons are at fault and one or more of them is or are responsible for damage while the other or others is or are free from causal responsibility, but it is not possible to establish which is the case, such two or more persons shall be deemed to be concurrent wrongdoers in respect of the damage."

This allows for liability to be imposed on all defendants at fault even where it cannot be established which caused the injury.

LEGAL CAUSATION: REMOTENESS OF DAMAGE

The principles of remoteness determine the cut off point of liability for damage, in other words, they decide whether the resulting injury will be compensated. The defendant is always liable for damage caused which was intentional, intention is said to "dispose of any question of remoteness of damage". Liability for unintentional damage (the vast majority of tort cases) is more contentious. An earlier "directness" test which held the defendant liable for all injury which flowed from the tortious act has now been almost completely discounted in favour of the "foreseeable injury test". This test only finds the defendant liable for those types of injuries that could be foreseen. However, the liberal interpretation of "foreseeability" by the courts in some cases has meant that the remoteness question is more one of policy than of any clear principles of law.

Liability for Direct Consequences Test

This test rather unfairly held that a defendant would be liable for all the consequences which flowed from his or her tortious act, regardless of how unlikely those consequences were. The case most associated with this test is that of *Polemis and Furness Withy & Co Ltd, Re* [1921] 3 K.B. 560 (*Re Polemis*). The facts are somewhat complicated. An agent of the defendants negligently knocked a plank into the hold of a ship. The impact caused a spark which ignited petrol vapour leading to an explosion. This in turn caused a fire destroying the ship. The owners of the ship brought an action against the charterers for the damage caused. The argument that the damage was too remote was put forward, in that knocking a plank could not lead reasonably to the conclusion that a ship would be destroyed. The court rejected this argument stating that so long as some damage was foreseeable, then the defendants would be liable for all damage arising out of the action. As stated by Scrutton L.J. "... if the act would or might reasonably cause damage, the fact that the damage it in fact causes is not the exact kind of damage one would expect is immaterial, so long as the damage is in fact directly traceable to the negligent act ..."

This test was never fully adopted in Ireland and was finally overruled by the decision in *Overseas Tankship (UK) Ltd v Morts Doct & Engineering Co (The Wagon Mound) No.1* [1961] A.C. 388, which gave way to the "liability for foreseeable injury" test.

Liability for Foreseeable Injury

The leading authority on this test is that of *Wagon Mound (No.1)*. In the case of *Wagon Mound* the defendants carelessly allowed some oil to spill into Sydney Harbour. About six hours later the oil flowed to a nearby wharf where some other ships were undergoing repairs. The plaintiffs continued welding on the wharf believing it was safe to do so. Some 60 hours later the welding appears to have ignited a rag in the water which led to the oil going on fire. This fire severely damaged the wharf and interfered with the plaintiff's use of the wharf. The Privy Council rejected the validity of *Re Polemis*, stating that this test placed an undue burden on tortfeasors. The new position was enunciated by Viscount Simonds as follows "... the essential factor in determining liability is whether the damage is of such a kind as the reasonable man should have foreseen." As the fire was not deemed to be foreseeable (in fact this point had not been argued by the plaintiffs) liability for it was not imposed. Significant doubt had already been cast on the "direct consequences" test about 10 months earlier in the Irish case of *O'Mahony v Ford & Son* [1962] I.R. 146. Referring to an even earlier finding in *Carey v The Cork Consumer Gas Company*, Supreme Court, March 5, 1958, the Supreme Court, in a rejection of the test in *Re*

Polemis, held that an employer could not be liable for injury of a type (in this case cancer) that could not be foreseen.

The courts do not require that the exact *manner* in which the injury arises is foreseeable, only that the injury itself is.

Type of Injury

As stated above the injury must not only be foreseeable but must be of a type that is foreseeable. But how is one type of injury distinguishable from another? The courts have never definitively decided this question. It appears to require something more that simply belonging to a category of damage such as physical, psychological or economic damage. Cancer will not be the same type of damage as bruising (*O'Mahony*) but a hernia (caused by extreme straining of muscles) is of the same type as muscle strain (*Burke v John Paul & Co Ltd* [1967] I.R. 277). The determination of "type" appears to enjoy a wide latitude. In this sense it is sometimes argued that it does not differ too greatly from the "direct consequences test." Some writers argue that the principle enjoys such flexibility that it appears that the courts simply use it to find as they wish in a particular case.

Egg-shell Skull Rule

In some cases the extent of damage may be much greater than expected due to some weakness on the part of the plaintiff. The defendant will still be held liable however, reflecting the principle that "the tortfeasor takes his victim as he finds him", a principle also referred to as the "egg-shell skull" rule. A defendant will therefore be liable where a leg is shattered as opposed to broken because of the plaintiff's osteoporosis, or where a plaintiff suffers severe back injury as opposed to simple back strain because of a pre-existing back condition. This principle was also applied in the case of *Burke v John Paul & Co Ltd* [1967] I.R. 277. The plaintiff developed a hernia following the use of a blunt hand-operated cutting machine for cutting steel. The defendants accepted that while they could foresee that some injury might arise (in the nature of tearing of muscles for instance) they argued that the development of a hernia could not be foreseen. The court held that the case was caught under the "egg-shell skull" rule and as the defendants could foresee some physical injury in the form of muscle strain, they were obliged to take the plaintiff as they found him and were liable for the resulting hernia.

This principle also extends to situations when the weakness is an economic as opposed to a physical one (although an exception to this general rule appears to apply in England (*Liesbosch Dredger v Edison SS* [1933] A.C. 448)). In a number of cases the courts have held that a defendant is obliged to bear the extra cost brought about as a result of a plaintiff's impecuniosity. So for instance, if as a result of negligently caused damage to a plaintiff's car, that plaintiff must borrow money to hire another one, the defendant is not only liable for cost of the car rental but also for any interest payable on the loan. Similarly in *Riordan's Travel Ltd v Acres and Co Ltd (No. 2)* [1979] I.L.R.M. 3, the defendants were liable not only for damage to the building and loss of profits but also for interest arising out of a need to borrow money to rent new premises.

3. NEGLIGENCE

INTRODUCTION

The tort of negligence is by far the most common tort on which litigation in our courts is based. It is one of the most recent torts, the earlier common law being almost exclusively concerned with the intentional wrongdoer, or with narrow specific incidents of duty and breach. At one time an injured person would have to sue in contract or by some other means if they wished to be compensated, a general tort of negligence with its own distinct set of principles did not begin to emerge until the 1800s.

To succeed in a negligence action a plaintiff must satisfy a number of conditions. First, the plaintiff must show that the defendant(s) owed a duty of care. Secondly, the plaintiff must establish that the defendant(s) fell below a reasonable standard of care (i.e. that the defendant was negligent). Generally speaking it is for the plaintiff to prove that the defendant was negligent. The only exception to this is when the negligence of the defendant is clear, in which case negligence is presumed and it is for the defendant to rebut this presumption (the principle of *res ipsa loquitur*). Thirdly, the defendant must establish causation (see Chapter 2).

This chapter will discuss the guidelines developed by the courts to determine to whom a duty is owed, the standard and its breach, and the principle of *res ipsa loquitur*.

DUTY OF CARE

Early Case Law

The first major case in the development of the "duty of care test" was that of *Donoghue v Stevenson* [1932] A.C. 562. The facts were that the plaintiff suffered shock and a bout of gastro-enteritis after having consumed a bottle of ginger beer, which she alleged were caused by the discovery of a decomposed snail at the bottom of the bottle (this was never established). The question arose as to whether she could pursue a claim against the manufacturers of the ginger ale. While it is clear today that she could recover, at the time the traditional view was that a contract relationship had to exist before a person could claim.

(Consider the view of Lord Abinger in 1842 who foresaw that the "most absurd and outrageous consequences, to which I can see no limit, would ensue", should anyone owe a duty to another outside of the scope of privity of contract, *Winterbottom v Wright* (1842) 10 M. & W. 109 at 114). The novelty of holding a manufacturer liable for possible damage to all end users was so innovative that the final judgment of the court was split, three of the five judges finding for the plaintiff and two against. The view of the majority based their decision on the principle that a duty of care is owed to your "neighbour". As to who was your "neighbour", Lord Aiken stated the following:

> "The rule that you must love your neighbour becomes in law you must not injure your neighbour; and the lawyer's question, who is my neighbour?, receives a restricted reply. You must take reasonable care to avoid acts or omissions which you can reasonably foresee would be liable to injure your neighbour. Who, then, in law, is my neighbour? The answer seems to be—persons who are so closely and directly affected by my act that I ought reasonably to have them in contemplation as being so affected when I am directing my mind to the acts or omissions which are called in question."

Otherwise put, a person owes a duty to anyone they can reasonably foresee that they could injure either by their acts or omission. This definition was ultimately accepted as the first definitive test of when a duty of care was owed. It could thus be applied to develop new "duty situations" which had not hitherto been recognised. Lord Aiken himself was not entirely comfortable with a general principle which could be used to determine who was owed a duty of care stating that "To seek a complete logical definition of the general principle is probably to go beyond the function of the judge, for the more general the definition the more likely it is to omit essentials or to introduce non essentials."

This test was developed a number of years later in the case of *Anns v Merton Urban District Council* [1978] A.C. 728. Here Lord Wilberforce in developing the "neighbour principle" put forward his two-tier test:

> "First, one has to ask whether, as between the alleged wrong-doers and the person who has suffered damage there is a

sufficient relationship of proximity or neighbourhood such that, in the reasonable contemplation of the former, careless- ness on his part may be likely to cause damage to the latter, in which case a prima facie duty of care arises. Secondly, if the first question is answered affirmatively, it is necessary to consider whether there are any considerations which ought to negative, or to reduce or limit the scope of the duty or the class of person to whom it is owed or the damages to which a breach of it may give rise."

This test went further that that of Lord Aiken's above. First, to the requirement of reasonable foreseeability was added a relationship of proximity between the plaintiff and the defendant. This relationship of "proximity" could be in time, space or could be a relationship of legal proximity. Secondly, if this test was satisfied the court must then consider whether any reasons exist (policy reasons or otherwise) so as not to recognize a duty of care in that particular case.

Duty of Care: Current English Position

In England there developed widespread dissatisfaction with the principles discussed above throughout the 1980s, opponents arguing that they lacked precision and could lead to a situation where in the words of Lord Templeman (*Songs v Amstrad* [1988] A.C. 1013) "The pleading assumes we are all neighbours now, Pharisees and Samaritans alike, that fore-seeability is a reflection of hindsight and that for every mischance in an accident-prone world someone must be liable in damages."

Others, such as Lord Oliver, in *Alcock v Constable* [1991] 3 W.L.R. 1057, were dissatisfied with the vagueness of the concept of proximity which Lord Oliver described as "an artificial one which depends more upon the Court's perception of what is the reasonable area for the imposition of liability that upon any logical process of analogical deduction."

This criticism was fueled by a fear that the "neighbour principle" was expanding too rapidly in developing liability for novel categories of loss guided only by issues of foreseeability of harm and to a lesser extent policy considerations. Judicial caution resurfaced and the courts sought to retreat to an approach which only allowed new categories of duty to develop incrementally. It became clear that not only would the courts require foreseeability and proximity but they would also require reasons why it would be "just and reasonable" to impose a duty on the defendant. The leading case in signaling the rejection of the two-tier approach in *Anns* and a move to more cautious incrementalist approach was that of *Caparo Industries Plc v Dickman* [1990] 2 A.C. 605. In this case the claimants sought to recover for losses sustained after relying on an incorrect evaluation of a company they subsequently invested in. The House of Lords found that in this case no duty of care was owed. Lord Bridge was clearly of the view that a general principle of foreseeability should not longer be used to determine whether a duty of care existed stating that "It is preferable, in my view, that the law should develop novel categories of negligence incrementally and by analogy with established categories ...". Ultimately the court in rejecting the earlier tests laid down their own three-step test which required foreseeability, proximity and that the imposition of a duty would be "just and reasonable". This third criterion would essentially allow the courts to restrict the unfettered expansion of the duty of care to new situations.

Duty of Care: Irish position

In Ireland the two-step test initiated in *Donoghue* and developed in *Anns* remained that accepted by our courts until the 2002 decision of *Glencar Exploration Plc v Mayo County Council* [2002] 1 I.R. 84. This case heralded not so much a rejection by the Supreme Court of the two-step test but more an adaptation of it in favour of the incrementalist approach currently applied in England. Prior to this decision the *Anns* test had been quoted with approval in a number of cases from *McNamara v ESB* [1975] I.R. 1 to *Ward v McMaster* [1988] I.R. 337. In the *Ward* case McCarthy J. stated that the duty of care arose from the proximity of the parties, the foreseeability of the damage, balanced against the "absence of any compelling exemption based upon public policy." However he added that any policy consideration would have to be a very powerful one if it were to "be used to deny an injured party his right to redress at the expense of the person or body who injured him." The decisions in *Glencar* and in *Fletcher v Commissioners of Public Works* [2003] 2 I.L.R.M. 94, (see Chapter 8) have demonstrated a retreat from this position.

In *Glencar*, the plaintiffs, a mining exploration company, had invested heavily in mining in Mayo. Mayo County Council introduced a mining ban leading to significant losses for the plaintiffs. It turned out subsequently that Mayo County Council had acted ultra vires and the plaintiffs sued in negligence to recover their losses. Keane C.J. in considering whether a duty of care arose, examined the test to be applied. He questioned whether in fact the two-step test was the correct test to follow in this jurisdiction, stating that:

> "There is, in my view, no reason why courts determining whether a duty of care arises should consider themselves obliged to hold that it does in every case where injury or damage to property was reasonably foreseeable and the notoriously difficult and elusive test of '*proximity*' or '*neighbourhood*' can be said to have been met, unless very powerful public policy considerations dictate otherwise. It seems to me that no injustice will be done if they are required to take the further step of considering whether, in all the circumstances, it is just and reasonable that the law should impose a duty ..."

Essentially the effect of *Glencar* is to add a third step to the two-step test adopted in *Anns,* i.e. whether it is "just and reasonable" to impose a duty of care and is more sympathetic to the incrementalist approach favoured by the English courts. In *Gaffey v Dundalk Town Council* [2006] I.E.H.C. 436 Peart J. applied the three-stage test of duty of care in *Glencar* in finding that it would not be reasonable to impose a duty on the defendant council in relation to fire hydrants in the town (given that there were 2500 such hydrants and no previous complaints in relation to them).

Immunity from suit

Certain categories of people have been held to have immunity from litigation when acting in the course of their profession, this is deemed to be necessary for the public good. This has been applied to barristers (*Rondel v Worsley* [1969] A.C. 191), judges, those who participate in trials, the Attorney General and statutory tribunals (*Beatty v Rent Tribunal* [2005] I.E.S.C. 66, although in this case Fennelly J. preferred to frame it not in terms of immunity but rather as it not being "just and reasonable" to impose a duty). However in England, the immunity of barristers appears to have been removed in civil cases at least (*Hall v Simons* [2000] 3 W.L.R. 543). It is yet to be seen what the position will be in Ireland.

Acts and omissions

While the law of negligence requires us not to injure our neighbour by our acts or omissions this has largely meant that we must not actively harm someone who is our neighbour (misfeasance). On the other hand the law has not traditionally required us to act to protect our neighbour either, there is therefore no duty to come to the aid of someone in danger (no breach of duty for failure to act (nonfeasance)). The law has recognised some exceptions to this general rule so that an affirmative duty of care is imposed if we fail to act in the following cases:

1. Where the relationship in question gives rise to a duty (e.g. failure of a parent to care for their child; failure of a prison to protect inmates; failure of an employer to protect the health and safety of employees).
2. Where the defendant has created the peril (in this case the defendant would be under a duty to act to prevent harm to others, *Bates v Minister for Justice*, Supreme Court, March 4, 1998).
3. Where a danger exists in relation to something which the defendant controls, in which case there may be a duty to warn (e.g. duty to warn of dangers on property; a duty of manufacturers or service providers to warn of dangers in products).

STANDARD OF CARE

An action in negligence requires not only that the plaintiff owes the defendant a duty of care but also that the defendant falls below the standard of the "reasonably careful man". As stated in *McComiskey v McDermott* [1974] I.R. 75 at 89 "The law of negligence lays down that the standard of care is that which is to be expected from a reasonably careful man in the circumstances." While this in theory is a constant and objective standard in practice it is largely subjective. It requires the court to take into account not only the nature and capacity of the litigants in question but also the circumstances of the case itself.

It is worth bearing in mind that statute also lays down certain standards that are expected in a given situation, in this way the Occupiers Liability Act 1995 lays down the standard owed to entrants onto property, while other pieces of legislation deal with the area of health and safety, traffic violations, and employers' liability.

The "reasonable man"

The reasonable man has at times been referred to as the man of ordinary prudence, the man on the Clapham omnibus, or the man on the Bondi tram. In Ireland the "reasonable man" was discussed in the case of *Kirby v Burke & Holloway* [1944] I.R. 207. In this case the plaintiffs purchased from the defendants a pot of rhubarb and ginger jam. It transpired that the jam was infected and caused those of the Kirby family who ate it to suffer from bouts of gastroenteritis. In finding the manufacturer liable for negligently allowing flies to get into the jam, Gavan Duffy J. stated the following:

> "... the foundation of liability at common law is blame-worthiness as determined by the existing average standards of the community; a man fails at his peril to conform to those standards. Therefore, while loss from accident generally lies where it fall, a defendant cannot plead accident if, treated as a man of ordinary intelligence and foresight, he ought to have foreseen the danger which caused injury to his plaintiff."

The law does not require perfection, as the person of ordinary intelligence himself is not perfect. On the other hand to say that one has done one's best is not enough, if that is not up to the standard of the reasonable person given that person's capacities.

The effect of the knowledge of the nature of the act is best summed up by the following statement by Kingsmill Moore J. in the case of *Byrne v McDonald*, Supreme Court, February 7, 1957 "... if there is, or should be, no knowledge that the act or omission involves danger, the plaintiff cannot be convicted for failing to take reasonable care." This is however qualified in that "... every adult is imputed the knowledge of risks which the normal reasonable person may be assumed to have ...". On the other hand, those who hold themselves up to have specialised knowledge, such as doctors and lawyers, will be expected to act in a manner commiserate with that knowledge.

A person with physical incapacities will not be expected to behave as if he were completely able bodied. This does not however, mean that a person who is incapacitated will be allowed to behave as they wish. It involves a balance between allowing the physically incapacitated a reasonable degree of freedom and on the other hand protecting against accidents. Thus a blind person will not be excused if they drive and cause an accident but they will be permitted to cross the street where there is some risk of impeding traffic. In such a case the standard appears to be that of a reasonable person suffering from that particular disability. In the case of *S.A. Ambulance v Walheim* (1948) 77 C.L.R. 7, for instance, a man with defective hearing was absolved from contributory negligence for failing to hear and ambulance siren. However, in the case of *O'Brien v Parker* [1997] 2 I.L.R.M. 170 liability was imposed on the defendant when he suffered an epileptic fit while driving as notwithstanding that he had never suffered such an attack before, he had admitted to feeling unwell that morning.

The extent to which mental incapacity informs liability is unresolved in Irish law. The courts have appeared to deal with the issue primarily from the point of view of the plaintiff as opposed to the defendant. One such case was that of *Armstrong v Eastern Health Board,* High Court, October 5, 1990, where a patient fell from a building after having received inadequate medical care. It was argued by the defence that she should at least be found liable in part as she had contributed to the injury. However, the court refuted this argument as Egan J. held that "she was not really in control of her thoughts" at the time.

"In the circumstances"

In considering the circumstances that must be taken into account in determining whether the defendant behaved reasonably the courts have focused on the following elements:

- Probability of the accident,
- Gravity of the threatened injury,
- Social utility of the defendant's conduct,
- Cost of eliminating the risk.

None of these considerations is definitive in itself but is balanced against the others in the determination of negligent behaviour.

Probability of the Accident

The greater the probability of an accident occurring the greater the standard of care imposed on the defendant. This is an entirely subjective exercise, the same act or omission may be negligent in one situation but not in another. The standard of care required when driving by a school for instance will be greater than that required when driving on the motorway; the duty not to smoke will be greater near a petrol pump than in your own car. In *O'Gorman v Ritz (Clonmel) Ltd* [1947] Ir. Jur. Rep. 35 the cinema owners were not found liable for injury to a patron given the low probability of such an injury arising. The plaintiff had sustained a minor injury when the person who had been sitting in the row in front of her got up, causing the seat in front to hit against her shins. The injury later became septic requiring treatment over a period of two months. Geoghegan J. held as follows:

"I am satisfied on the particular facts, that to guard against a remote contingency such as that which led to the injuries here would need precautions of a well-nigh fantastic nature, which could not reasonably be expected in the construction or management of a theater."

Gravity of the Threatened Injury

The more serious the foreseeable injury the greater the standard of care required. So for instance the degree of care which must be taken in transporting toxic or otherwise dangerous materials such as gas, oil, or nuclear fuel, would be much greater than that required when transporting vegetables. Being hit by a carrot, while unfortunate, is not likely to maim you in any serious fashion. The knowledge imported to an individual as to the gravity of the injury is that which the defendant had or that a reasonable person would have in those circumstances.

Social Utility of the Defendant's Conduct

The utility of the conduct itself must be balanced against the gravity and probability of the risk. In this way ambulances can drive at great speed through traffic due to the urgency of their errand while on the other hand a person rushing home to catch the beginning of a football match could not. Similarly, we tolerate rally driving where it could injure those nearby, or golfers where they could injure spectators, given the social utility of sporting events. What is required is that reasonable care is taken given the circumstances of the case. As with the gravity of the injury, one act may be excused where it is done for a laudable purpose and will not where it has no such justification. In *Whooley v Dublin Corporation* [1961] I.R. 60 for instance, the plaintiff tripped and sustained an injury by putting her foot through an open hydrant box when she was walking along a footpath in Dublin. The lid of the box, which should have been attached, had been removed by a passerby. The question arose as to whether Dublin Corporation was liable in not making the box more secure and inaccessible for passersby. The court looked to the social utility of the act, the hydrant box had been left in that position so as to facilitate access to it by fire officers. To remove it to a more in accessible location would be to jeopardise any future firefighting activity. Thus the court found no negligence. In the words of McLoughlin J. "no other fire hydrant which could be devised, consistent with its necessary purpose, would be safe from … malicious interference."

Cost of Eliminating the Risk

The risk created must be balanced against the cost of removing the risk. Generally speaking if the cost of removing the risk is high, and the probability of the risk low, then no liability will fall. So for instance in the case of *Callaghan v Killarney Race Co Ltd* [1958] I.R. 366 where injury arose from a horse crashing through a fence at the position of a hurdle, no liability arose. It was held by the Supreme Court that to extend the protective fence around the perimeter would impose an expense that might well "put an end to many of the smaller race-course, or involve a higher price for admission." With respect to spillages, the liability imposed on larger supermarkets appears to be quite high. In the case of *Mullen v Quinnsworth t/a crazy Prices (No. 1)* [1990] 1 I.R. 59 liability was imposed for failure to keep the floor clear of spillages. On the other hand in the case of *McSweeney v Garda Siochána Boat Club,* High Court, June 5, 1991, liability was not imposed where an injury arose due to drinks being spilled on the dance floor. In this case the court was satisfied that a reasonable system had been put in place to ensure that they were mopped up immediately and the court felt that the spillage in this case could not have been there for longer than a few minutes.

RES IPSA LOQUITUR

Generally speaking the burden of proof in showing negligence falls on the plaintiff and it is not for the defendant to disprove anything. There is however, an exception in the principle of *res ipsa loquitur* ("the thing speaks for itself"). It arises in cases where damage has been caused to the plaintiff in circumstances in which it could not reasonably have arisen without negligence on the part of the defendant.

Once *res ipsa* is said to apply the burden of proof is reversed and it falls on the defendant to show that he or she was not negligent.

One of the earliest cases to outline the principle was that of *Scott v London & St. Katherine Docks Co* (1865) 3 H & C 722. In this case the plaintiff was struck by bags of sugar which fell from a warehouse controlled by the defendants. The court held that this was a case where the principle of *res ipsa loquitur* could be applied. The court described such cases as follows:

> "There must be reasonable evidence of negligence. But where the thing is shown to be under the management of the defendant or his servants, and the accident is such that in the ordinary circumstances does not happen if ... management use proper care, it affords reasonable evidence, in the absence of explanation by the defendants, that the accident arose from want of care."

The "thing" which causes the accident must be under the defendant's management or control, but this concept should be broadly understood to include past control or alternatively the right to control, where this is appropriate. In the case of *Collen Brothers (Dublin) Ltd v Scaffolding Ltd* [1959] I.R. 254 for instance, the defendants who supplied scaffolding to the plaintiffs which subsequently collapsed were held to have the scaffolding under "their management" and control even though it was at the time being used by the plaintiffs.

The event must also be one which would not have occurred in the ordinary course of events without some negligence on the part of the defendant. Instances where the principle has been applied include the case of an eight year old girl falling into a coma during an appendix operation (*Lindsay v Mid-Western Health Board* [1993] 2 I.R. 147), animals straying from a fenced area onto the highway (*O'Shea v Tilman Anhold and Horse Holiday Farm Ltd,* unreported, Supreme Court, Hamilton C.J., O'Flaherty, Keane JJ., October 23, 1996) and a syringe being left on a seat in a train carriage injuring a young girl (*Boyle v Eireann/Irish Rail,* Circuit Court, January 30, 2006).

If the principle is applied it is then open to the defendant to rebut the presumption of negligence either by showing how the injury came about or by proving that they had taken all reasonable care.

4. ECONOMIC LOSS

INTRODUCTION

Traditionally the courts have had no difficulty in allowing recovery for economic loss sustained due to some personal injury or property damage. However, they have been consistently more reluctant to allow recovery for pure economic loss (financial loss which is not causally consequent on physical injury). The current position in England is that such loss is not recoverable outside of the confines of the tort of negligent misstatements (see below). The position in Ireland is less clear. The Irish courts initially did not allow recovery for pure economic loss but later tempered this position by stating that they did not see any difficulty in allowing recovery. More recently, the decision in *Glencar Exploration Plc v Mayo County Council* [2002] 1 I.R. 84 has again cast doubt over whether recovery for pure economic loss is possible.

WHY THE RELUCTANCE?

The traditional view has been that pure economic loss should be recoverable through contractual relations only and that to allow tort to venture into this area confuses the distinction between them. It is also argued that to require a defendant to pay for economic loss, the extent of which might not be foreseeable, would be to place too great a burden on potential defendants. Take for instance a person who cuts the electricity supply to a nearby town, if recovery for pure economic loss was allowed that person could conceivably be liable for the loss of profits of all businesses in that town. As stated in the case of *Hedley Byrne & Co Ltd v Heller and Partners* [1964] A.C. 465 "It may be that the size and the width of the range of possible claims has acted as a deterrent to extension of economic protection."

An accepted exception to the general rule has existed since the *Hedley Byrne* decision in 1964 which allowed recovery for pure economic loss arising from negligent misstatements. The proximity requirement of this tort is strictly defined however, which limits the number of claimants who could potentially recover.

RECOVERING FOR ECONOMIC LOSS

English Position

The earliest cases in both England and in Ireland allowed recovery for consequential economic loss but were clearly against finding for the plaintiff in incidences of pure economic loss. In the English decision of *Cattle v Stockton Waterworks* (1875) LR 10 Q.B. 453 the plaintiffs were working on land which the defendants negligently flooded. The plaintiffs sued for their economic loss as they were delayed in finishing the work they were carrying out. The court did not allow recovery on the basis that their loss was economic only. On the other hand economic loss consequential on physical loss was clearly recoverable. In the English case of *S.C.M. v Whittall* [1971] 1 Q.B. 337 a building contractor caused damage to overhead cables leading to a loss of electricity to a nearby factory. This in turn caused damage to both machinery and materials, and lead to a consequent loss of productivity. Lord Denning in his decision stated:

> "It is well settled that when a defendant by his negligence causes physical damage to the person or property of the plaintiff, in such circumstances that the plaintiff is entitled to compensation for the physical damage, then he can claim, in addition, for economic loss consequent on it ... In actions of negligence, when the plaintiff has suffered no damage to his person or property, but has only sustained economic loss, the law does not usually permit him to recover that loss. The reason lies in public policy."

The decision of *Junior Books Ltd v Veitchi* [1983] 520 (HL) cast doubt over whether this strict approach still applied in England. In this case the owners of a factory sued the defendants who were responsible for a defective floor being laid in their factory. The floor did not cause any physical or personal damage but replacing the floor led to a loss of profits on the part of the plaintiffs. The House of Lords held that the fact that the loss was economic only was not a bar to recovery and they referred the case back to the original court for resolution. Subsequent case law in England has indicated that *Junior Books* should be restricted to the facts of that case (i.e. close proximity, reliance on skill and only one claimant) and is not authority for the general position that recovery for pure economic loss is allowed. It remains to be seen how the courts will deal with such cases in the future but it is likely that recovery for pure economic loss will continue to be tightly controlled.

Irish Case Law

Ireland's earliest decisions, as in England, were clearly hostile to a right to recover for pure economic loss. In *Irish Paper Sacks Ltd v John Sisk & Son (Dublin) Ltd,* High Court, May 18, 1972, for instance, the fact that the only loss sustained was economic barred recovery. In this case the defendants severed an electricity cable while digging on the highway. This resulted in a loss of electricity to the plaintiff's factory for two days during which production ceased. There was no physical damage as the cable was not on the plaintiff's property but there was economic loss due to lost labour, overheads and profit. In this case O'Keefe P. stated that "… a plaintiff suing for damages suffered as a result of an act or omission of the defendant cannot recover if the act or omission did not directly injure the plaintiff's person or property, but merely caused consequential loss."

More recently however, the courts have held that recovery hinges on the issues of proximity and foreseeability and that the nature of the loss (physical or economic) is irrelevant (see for instance McCarthy J., in *Ward v McMaster* [1989] I.L.R.M. 400). The *Ward* case allowed recovery to the plaintiff who had bought a defective house from the defendant builder/vendor. Another often recited case supporting recovery for pure economic loss is that of *McShane Wholesale Fruit & Vegetables Ltd v Johnston Haulage Co Ltd* [1997] 1 I.L.R.M. 86. In this case a fire which started in the defendant's premises spread to the plaintiff's premises, causing the electricity supply to the plaintiff's fruit and vegetables business to be cut off. They sustained economic loss as a result and the court allowed them to recover. As stated by Flood J. in the *McShane* case, an action "will not fail because the damage is of a particular type" but because of a lack of proximity or foreseeability between the parties.

However, it is arguable that Ireland has not had a successful case involving pure economic loss outside of the area of negligent misstatement, in which case any comment on such recovery by the Irish courts is merely obiter. For instance in both *Ward* and *McShane* some physical damage occurred. In the latter case it appeared that the fire had spread to the plaintiff's premises although the plaintiff only appears to have sued for economic loss arising from the loss of electricity.

One of the most recent significant cases to comment on the issue is that of *Glencar* where Keane C.J. stated that notwithstanding the judgment in *Ward* it was still unclear whether recovery for pure economic loss was allowed in this jurisdiction outside of the area of negligent misstatement. The former Chief Justice also questioned whether the *Junior Books* decision ought to be followed in Ireland. This ambiguity in relation to the Irish position was also evident in *Beatty v Rent Tribunal* [2005] I.E.S.C. where Geoghegan J. stated "I am satisfied that the law on this question has not been finally determined in Ireland notwithstanding some relevant *obiter dicta* of Keane C.J. in *Glencar Explorations p.l.c. v. Mayo County Council (No. 2)* [2002] 1 I.R. 84." These statements casts significant doubt over whether any general right to recovery for pure economic loss exists in Ireland.

ECONOMIC LOSS AND NEGLIGENT MISSTATEMENTS (*HEDLEY BYRNE* PRINCIPLE)

The one area where recovery for pure economic loss has been allowed is in the case of negligent misstatements. Recovery is decided on the basis of the traditional negligence principles of proximity and foreseeability with a particular emphasis on the requirement for close proximity between the parties. The first case which allowed recovery in this area was that of *Hedley Byrne & Co Ltd v Heller and Partners* [1964] A.C. 465. Prior to this decision recovery had only been allowed where there existed either a fiduciary or contractual relationship between the parties.

In this case the plaintiffs, an advertising company, asked their bank to contact their client's bank to ascertain their client's credit worthiness before embarking on some work for them. The work was to be carried out on credit. Relying on a favourable credit rating the plaintiffs carried out the work for their clients, and suffered a loss when they failed to pay. The court held that liability for negligent misstatement could arise where the following conditions were satisfied: clear reliance by the plaintiff on the statement made; reliance by the plaintiff being foreseeable and reasonable; and the existence of a special relationship between the parties (proximity). As all three existed in this case a duty of care arose. However, as the client's bank had asked for a disclaimer to be signed by the plaintiff's bank in relation to the information given, they were absolved of any wrongdoing in relation to it. Despite this the *Hedley Byrne* principle has formed the basis for a number of subsequent decisions supporting liability for negligent misstatements.

Hedley Byrne applied in Ireland

In Ireland the decision in *Hedley Byrne* has been followed in a line of cases. While initial case law would have supported the view that it was a subset of negligence it is clear from the decision in *Wildgust v Bank of Ireland and Norwich Union Life Assurance Society,* High Court, July 28, 1998, that a claim for negligent misstatement (and not simply negligence) must be clearly made out before it will be considered by the courts.

Proximity

As stated earlier the proximity requirement in negligent misstatements actions is tightly construed, being in fact closer to the relationship that arises in contract than that typically required to support a finding of a duty of care. If the advice is not given directly to the plaintiff intending it to be relied on by him or her it will be more difficult to establish the necessary degree of proximity (see *Securities Trust Ltd v Hugh Moore & Alexandra Ltd* [1964] I.R. 417 and *McSweeney v Burke*, High Court, November 24, 1980 below). In *Securities Trust* the plaintiff company, which relied on the Articles of Association of the defendant company, sued the defendants when a printing error in the Articles led them to suffer a financial loss. However, as the Articles had not been provided to the plaintiffs directly but to a Mr Anderson acting on their behalf, the court held that a sufficient relationship of proximity did not arise. As stated by Davitt P. "It can hardly be seriously contended that the defendant Company owed a duty to the world at large to take care to avoid mistakes and printers' errors in the reprint of their Articles."

A similar finding was made in *McSweeney* where advice given to a group of companies did not entitle individuals within that group to claim that it established proximity in relation to them personally. The court refused to find for the plaintiffs holding that the advice was to the group of companies stating, "I do not see how a third party who knows of the advice given to the client and who carries out steps outlined in that advice (ultimately to his own detriment) can claim that the advice was negligent in relation to him."

However, a more liberal interpretation of the proximity requirement was given in *Wildgust v Norwich Union Life Insurance Society* [2006] I.E.S.C. 19. In this case, Mr Wildgust had suffered a loss when Norwich Union refused to pay on his wife's life insurance policy, stating that it had lapsed. The lapse had occurred due to a false assurance by Norwich Union to a third party, Hill Samuel, that a missed payment had been met when in fact it had not. The Supreme Court, overturning the finding against the plaintiff in the High Court, held that despite the fact that the statement had not been made to Mr Wildgust he could recover for his loss. As stated by Kearns J., an interpretation of *Hedley Byrne* could include not just the person to whom the advice was addressed but "persons in a limited and identifiable class" where it is clear that they also relied on the information given.

Foreseeability

In addition to the proximity requirement it must be foreseeable that the plaintiff would rely on the statement and such reliance must be reasonable. In *Tulsk v Ulster Bank Ltd,* High Court, May 13, 1983 the defendants gave advice to the plaintiff (who was a customer) stating that another person, who was also their customer, was creditworthy when in fact they were not. The plaintiffs relied on the information and suffered a loss. Here Gannon J. imposed liability by finding that the bank knew or could foresee that the plaintiffs would rely on the information given, that the bank itself was in a position of having a special skill, and that the relationship was such between the bank and the plaintiff that such reliance was reasonable.

A case in which reliance was found to be unreasonable was that of *Gayson v Allied Irish Banks Ltd,* High Court, January 28, 2000. Here the plaintiff, who had availed of an offshore account as a means of avoiding tax, claimed that he had relied to his detriment on a statement made by a bank official to him that he need not take advantage of a tax amnesty available in 1988. Geoghegan J. found that the conversation in relation to the tax amnesty was of an "off the cuff" nature and that as banks generally were not in the "business of advising customers as to whether they should avail of a tax amnesty" reliance in this case was unreasonable. Significantly, Geoghegan J. also added that generally, if advice were given on two courses of action with one of them being illegal no actionable duty ought to arise without clear evidence that the plaintiff was unaware of the illegality involved.

5. PSYCHIATRIC DAMAGE (NERVOUS SHOCK)

INTRODUCTION

Nervous shock is the term used to describe mental injury on witnessing or being party to a traumatic event, usually an accident. The courts have not been enthusiastic in allowing recovery for this type of injury, partly as a result of skepticism of an injury that cannot be seen and a fear of encouraging limitless actions for metal injury (the floodgates argument). This reluctance has abated in recent years, due in part to advancements in medical science and greater social and judicial acceptance of mental injury claims. It is by no means absent from the courts however, with Kearns J. advocating a more restrictive Irish approach to those who could recover for nervous shock in *Cuddy v Mays* unreported, High Court, November 23, 2003 motivated by the fear of "exaggerated, or even fraudulent claims ...".

The courts in England and Ireland apply different principles when dealing with nervous shock claims, with the English courts imposing a more restrictive set of principles.

Each jurisdiction will be considered in turn. First, however, we must look at what constitutes nervous shock.

WHAT IS NERVOUS SHOCK?

Nervous shock has been defined as any medically recognised psychiatric illness or trauma which is brought about by a shock, generally on witnessing or being party to an accident or its aftermath. The injury must have been brought about negligently. The most common medically recognised illness of this type is post traumatic stress disorder (PTSD).

The plaintiff must be able to show that the illness was a result of a "shock" and not simply an accumulated effect from grief or loss. In *Kelly v Hennessy* [1995] 3 I.R. 253 the defendants unsuccessfully tried to argue that Mrs. Kelly's psychiatric injury was brought about as a result of the trauma of caring for her family as opposed to witnessing the aftermath of the accident in order to deny her a right to compensation.

In the recent decision of the Supreme Court in *Fletcher v Commissioners for Public Works* [2003] 2 I.L.R.M. 94, Keane C.J. criticized the logic of distinguishing between psychiatric injury arising from the event itself as opposed to suffering grief in its aftermath, stating that "it must surely be questionable whether the inflexible boundary drawn by the law between recognisable psychiatric conditions which are compensatable and grief or mental anguish, which is not, is entirely logical."

It is unclear however, whether the courts are willing to remove the current distinction or if they will simply await intervention on this issue by the legislature.

ENGLISH POSITION ON NERVOUS SHOCK

Traditionally the English courts have been reluctant to allow recovery for nervous shock, a reluctance which has been less prevalent in Ireland. In the case of *Victoria Ry Commrs v Coultas* (1888) 13 A.C. 222, a woman was denied recovery when she was almost hit by a train on the basis that allowing the claim would lead to "a wide field being opened for imaginary claims".

In recent years, as a further limitation on claims, the courts have drawn a distinction between primary and secondary victims.

One of the first cases to deal comprehensively with the issue in England was *McLoughlin v O'Brian* [1983] 1 A.C. 410. In this case the plaintiff's husband and three children were involved in a car crash. A motorist who had come on the immediate aftermath told the plaintiff of the accident after which she arrived at the hospital to witness severely distressing scenes. One of her children had died and the others were severely injured. The plaintiff suffered post traumatic stress disorder and while she was allowed to recover damages for nervous shock the Lords were divided as to their reasoning. Lords Russell, Scarman and Bridge applied the test of reasonable foreseeability, with Bridge deliberating on the issues of space, time and relationship in determining foreseeability. Issues of space, time and relationship were not legal requirements in themselves, only considerations in determining the degree of foreseeability of psychiatric injury.

On the other hand, Lords Wilberforce and Edmund-Davies held that to hold that foreseeability was the only requirement with no other policy restraints was to go a step too far. To that criterion must be added the requirement of strict proximity in time, a close relationship, and direct means of communication (personal witness). In terms of strict proximity in time it was held that a plaintiff would have to arrive at the scene of the accident or its aftermath shortly afterwards, although no specific time limit was set. Close family relationships would be covered and even an innocent bystander might recover if the other requirements were met. Finally, direct means of communication was required. Hearing about it from someone else without personally witnessing events would not suffice. Simultaneous communication by television was something to be considered by future courts.

Initially the view of Lord Bridge held sway, *Attia v British Gas* [1988] Q.B. 304; however, Lord Wilberforce's argument gathered credence in the case of *Alcock v Chief Constable of South Yorkshire* [1992] 1 A.C. 310.

The *Alcock* Case

The *Alcock* case arose out of the Hillsborough disaster in 1989 where 95 people were crushed to death and over 400 physically injured due to an overcrowded football stadium. This was clearly attributable to the negligence of the South of Yorkshire police who had allowed the overcrowding to take place.

The House of Lords in their decision drew a distinction between two types of claimants: primary victims and secondary victims. Primary victims included those actually in danger, those who perceived themselves to be in danger, and rescuers. Such claimants would succeed so long as they could show that psychiatric injury was foreseeable to a person of reasonable fortitude. Secondary victims were "non-participants" i.e. those who believed themselves to be in no personal danger. These would include those who witnessed the event, or heard about it either at the time or later. In order to succeed in a claim these secondary victims must satisfy the Wilberforce test as laid down in *McLoughlin,* i.e. foreseeability and a close tie of love and affection with the immediate victim, proximity in time and space to the accident or its immediate aftermath and perception of the accident or its aftermath by sight or hearing.

Ten people brought a claim on the basis of nervous shock suffered. Eight of the 10 had seen the events on television or heard about it on the radio and were not allowed to recover as there had not been a direct perception of the accident by sight or hearing. The court, however, did not rule out the possibility that recovery would be allowed in exceptional cases of simultaneous transmission. As for the two plaintiffs who were at the event only one was deemed to have the necessary proximity. The second, although the brother of the victim, could not show that there were sufficiently close ties between them.

The decision was criticized for its harshness, particularly given the perceived ease with which rescuers, who had no ties with the victims, could succeed.

A later decision, that of *White v Chief Constable of the South Yorkshire Police* [1999] 2 A.C. 455 dealt specifically with rescuers, modifying the approach taken in *Alcock*. In this case police officers involved in the rescue operation following Hillsborough sought to recover for damage sustained. Lord Hoffman stated that a "rescuer plaintiff" could only be regarded as a primary victim where they had objectively exposed themselves to physical danger or reasonably believed that they were doing so. As part of Lord Hoffman's reasoning he opined that to allow rescuers who had not been subject to injury to recover, would be to open the floodgates to people who would join as rescuers in order to seek compensation.

IRISH POSITION ON NERVOUS SHOCK

The Irish courts have been more responsive in allowing recovery for nervous shock. At about the time that the English courts denied recovery to the plaintiff in *Coultas*, the Irish courts allowed recovery in two very similar cases. In *Byrne v Southern and Western Ry. Co. of Ireland,* Court of Appeal, February, 1884, the plaintiff, a superintendent of the telegraph office at Limerick Junction was allowed recovery for nervous shock when a train struck his office, although he had admitted that not a hair on his head had been touched. *Byrne* was later confirmed in the case of *Bell v G.N. Ry. Co.* 26 L.R. (Ir) 428. In this case Murphy J. stated that it was:

"… immaterial whether the injuries be called nervous shock, brain disturbance, mental injury or shock. The only questions to be considered, in my opinion, are: was the health or capacity of the plaintiff for the discharge of her duties and enjoyment of life affected by what occurred to here whilst in the carriage? Next, was this caused by the negligence of the defendants?"

In both cases discussed above the plaintiffs were clearly in physical danger but the Irish courts have been equally receptive where the plaintiff has only witnessed the event or its aftermath. In the case of *Mullally v Bus Eireann* [1992] I.L.R.M. 522, which was factually very similar to that of *McLoughlin* above, Denham J. found for the plaintiff, stating that there was "no policy in Irish law opposed to a finding of nervous shock, an old term covering post traumatic stress disorder. Indeed the Irish courts were one of the first to find that such an illness existed and was compensatable …". She based her finding on the ordinary criteria of reasonable foreseeability, with reference to Lord Bridge in *McLoughlin* above.

In *Kelly v Hennessy* [1995] 3 I.R. 253, the issue of nervous shock was addressed again. In this case the plaintiff's husband and two daughters were involved in a car accident, with the husband and one of the daughters suffering brain damage and the second daughter making a full recovery. The plaintiff had not witnessed the accident but went into shock and became very upset on being told of the accident by telephone and became further traumatized on visiting the hospital shortly afterwards. The Supreme Court affirmed the finding of Lavan J. in favour of the plaintiff. Denham J. found for the plaintiff focusing on the issue of proximity, stating that:

> "I am satisfied that a person with a close proximate relation-
> ship to an injured person, such as the plaintiff, who, while not
> a participant in the accident, hears of it very soon after and
> who visits the injured person as soon as practicable, and who
> is exposed to serious injuries of the primary victims in such a
> way as to cause a psychiatric illness, then she becomes a
> secondary victim to the accident."

Hamilton C.J. (with whom Egan J. concurred to form the majority) laid down the following criteria, which have become the standard test for nervous shock cases in this jurisdiction:

- The plaintiff must establish that they suffer from a recognisable psychiatric illness,
- The injury must be shock induced,
- The nervous shock must have been caused by the defendant's negligence,
- The nervous shock must be by reason of actual or apprehended physical injury to the plaintiff or another person,

- The plaintiff must show that the defendant owed a duty of care not to cause the reasonably foreseeable nervous shock. As regards this element Hamilton C.J. stated that the relationship between the plaintiff and the person injured must be close, but did not specify particular relationships.

This test has been confirmed in a number of subsequent cases including that of *Curran v Cadbury (Ireland) Ltd* [2000] 2 I.L.R.M. 343 and *Devlin v National Maternity Hospital* [2008] 1 I.L.R.M. 301.

The distinction between primary and secondary victims has not been embraced in Ireland although reference to primary/secondary victims has been made in some cases (see Denham J. *Kelly v Hennessy* and McMahon J. in *Curran v Cadbury*). The general tendency of the Irish courts in this respect is to acknowledge that the distinction is unhelpful while stopping short of completely rejecting it (e.g. *Fletcher v Commissioners of Public Works in Ireland* [2003] I.L.R.M. 94).

Nor have the Irish courts sought to restrict the category of claimants by requiring that the claimant has a particular relationship with the injured person but this may be changing. In *Cuddy v Mays* unreported, High Court, November 23, 2003, Kearns J. stated that:

"This Court would certainly support the proposition that policy considerations would dictate that the ambit of recoverability and the category of relationships entitled to successfully claim damages for nervous shock should be tightly restricted."

In that case, the plaintiff was a porter in a hospital who assisted in taking the injured from arriving ambulances. He quickly realized that the injured included close relatives (including two siblings and a cousin) and neighbours and subsequently suffered from post traumatic stress disorder. Kearns J. understandably found in his favour, but in addition to the criteria outlined in *Kelly* advocated a policy based restriction allowing recovery only to those with a "close proximate relationship" with the injured party akin to a family relationship.

6. OCCUPIERS' LIABILITY

INTRODUCTION

The area of occupiers' liability deals with the tort of negligence as it applies to injuries to entrants onto land. Historically, the protection offered to entrants onto property who incurred an injury did not benefit to the same extent as other areas of negligence by the principles of *Donoghue v Stevenson*. This was due in part to the fact that the rights of property owners were well developed at the time that *Donoghue v Stevenson* was decided through the seminal decision of *Indermaur v Dames* (1888) L.R. 1 C.P. 274. This decision coupled with the laissez faire approach which applied to property issues in the late 19th century, meant that the rights of entrants onto land was directly related to their benefit to the land owner. As such, classifications of entrants were used ranging from that of contractual invitees to trespassers, each with their own corresponding levels of protection. This remained the position for many years in Ireland before negligence principles began to be applied in the area, most notably through judgements such as that of *McNamara v ESB* [1975] I.R. 1. However these decisions, although clarifying the duty owed to trespassers, did lead to some confusion as to the duty owed to other categories of claimants and raised the duty owed to trespassers to that of "reasonable care". Through lobbying by interests groups such as farmers, concerned by the extent of the duty owed to trespassers, the whole area of occupiers' liability was overhauled by the Occupiers' Liability Act 1995. This Act now largely replaces the common law on occupiers' liability. The Act however, only deals with injury arising from dangers due to the state of the premises and not due to activities carried out on it. This means that if the injury arises from activities on the premises, the Act will not apply. Although not clearly stated in the Act it is to be presumed that the old common law will apply in these cases.

EARLIER COMMON LAW POSITION

Under the common law as it existed prior to the Occupiers' Liability Act 1995 entrants onto premises divided into four categories relative to their benefit to the land owner. Premises for the purpose of occupiers' liability is widely defined to include land or buildings but also platforms, grandstands, ships in dock, scaffolding, electricity pylons, and in a number of cases vehicles and other movables. The four categories were:

1. Contractual entrants,
2. Invitees,
3. Licensees, and
4. Trespassers.

Contractual Entrants

A contractual entrant is one who enters a premises on foot of a contract between the entrant and the occupier, e.g. those who enter a cinema, theater, sporting event or concert. The duty owed was determined by the terms of the contract. In the absence of express terms the courts implied a term that the occupier had to take reasonable care for the safety of the entrant.

Invitees

An invitee was an entrant who went onto the property with the consent of the occupier in circumstances where the occupier had a material advantage in the visit. As there was a financial or other economic benefit or the potential of financial benefit to the occupier from the visit, the entrant in this case was owed a reasonably high duty of care. Examples would include entrants to shops, bars, restaurants, employees and those visiting tourist attractions (*Thomas v Leitrim County Council* [1998] 2 I.L.R.M. 74).

The duty owed was lower than that owed to a contractual entrant. It extended to taking reasonable care to prevent injury due to an "unusual danger" which the occupier knows or ought to know of. If however, the occupier did not know or could not reasonably know of the "unusual" danger then no liability arose in the case of an injury. The danger also had to one which was not an obvious one or one that was common on that type of premises.

Licensees

Licensees were entrants who came onto the property with the occupier's permission (express or implied) but who conferred no material benefit on the occupier (e.g. social guests, tolerated entrants (such as children), worshippers in a church, those entering parks and pupils at school.) The duty owed to licensees was limited to warning the licensee of concealed dangers of which the occupier was actually aware. Concealed meant in this context that the danger would not be reasonably appreciated by the plaintiff in question. It could mean something which is not readily visible, for instance a covered hole, or it could mean something visible but not appreciated by the plaintiff, due to the plaintiff's age or mental capacity.

Trespassers

A trespasser is an entrant who comes onto property with no express or implied right to be there or who remains on property after their right to be there has elapsed. Initially the occupier owed no duty to a person coming onto the premises as a trespasser, except not to do any act (misfeasance) intended to injure or was so reckless as to be likely to injure the trespasser, whose presence was known or ought to have been known by the occupier. A number of cases involving child trespassers led to a relaxation of this duty and in the case of *McNamara v ESB* [1975] I.R. 1 the court went so far as to impose a duty of reasonable care on the defendant where the presence of children was foreseeable, notwithstanding their status as trespassers. Essentially the duty owed to trespassers was in certain circumstances now elevated to that owed to a contractual entrant.

In addition there was some confusion over the duty owed to invitees and licensees. In the case of *Foley v Musgrave Cash and Carry Ltd*, Supreme Court, December 20, 1965 Griffin J. found for the plaintiff and stated that "In modern times it appears to me that the duty owed by the occupier to an invitee could best be said to be to take reasonable care in all the circumstances to see that the premises are reasonably safe for the invitee."

On the other hand in the later case of *Rooney v Connolly* [1967] I.L.R.M. 766 with respect to licensees the Supreme Court again used the terminology of "concealed danger". It was with this confused state with respect to invitees and licensees and in light of the now higher duty owed to trespassers that the enactment of the Occupiers' Liability Act 1995 came about.

OCCUPIERS' LIABILITY ACT 1995

The 1995 Act was a result of strong lobbying by farmers and other interest groups in the wake of the developments wrought by *McNamara* with respect to the duty owed to trespassers. While the Act is not without its critics there was little doubt that to regularise the situation regarding entrants was more favourable than letting the law develop to such an extent that an innocent occupier could be found liable for injuries sustained to any trespasser who happened to wander onto the occupier's land. The Act replaces the old common law in relation to the areas where the Act applies.

Scope of Duty

Liability under the Act replaces the old common law in relation to the liability of occupiers for dangers existing on premises. Danger however is defined narrowly, to cover only the state of the premises and not to activities carried out on it. Unfortunately, it is not always clear where the line between "activity" and "state" can be drawn. Say for instance that an occupier is in his field digging a hole and a passer by falls into the hole. Is this an injury arising out of the activity or the state of the premises? Likewise in the building of a wall, if someone trips over that wall is it a state or activity case? In the case of *McGovern v Dunnes Stores*, unreported, Circuit Court, McMahon J., March 6, 2003, the Circuit Court clarified what is meant by "state of premises". A customer in this case slipped on a clothes hanger lying on the floor. McMahon J. decided that as the incident did not relate to the "structural" state of the premises this was a case involving injury from activity and as such common law principles, rather than the 1995 Act, ought to be applied. In this case it did not raise any serious difficulties as the law relating to the duty to a visitor meant that the entrant was owed a duty of reasonable care (the highest possible had the Act been applied). In cases where the entrant might be classed as a "recreational user" or "trespasser" difficulties may well arise.

Occupier

The definition of occupier reflects that which existed in the common law. Section 1(1) states that an occupier is the person who controls as opposed to owns a premises. If there are a number of people who control the premises the extent of the duty of each occupier depends on their respective degrees of control.

Premises

Premises is also defined in light of its common law understanding. As such it includes land, water and any fixed or moveable structures thereon and also includes vessels, vehicles, trains (*Boyle v Eireann/ Irish Rail,* unreported, Circuit Court, McMahon J., January, 2006), aircraft and other means of transport.

New Classification of Entrants

The Act now refers to three categories of entrants:

1. Visitors,
2. Trespassers,
3. Recreational users.

Visitors

Visitors are defined as entrants who enter onto a premises with the express or implied right of the occupier, or those who are there as of right, or under contract and who are not recreational users. It also includes those who entered as visitors but no longer have permission to be there and are making reasonable efforts to leave. In terms of their relationship with the earlier common law categories visitors are those which were formerly classed as contractual entrants, invitees and licensees, excluding those which can be classed as "recreational users". Once a person exceeds their permission to be on the premises they become trespassers.

The duty owed to visitors is to take reasonable care in all the circumstances to ensure that they do not suffer injury or damage by reason of any danger existing on the property (s.3). Note must also be taken of the duty of any other person in the company of the entrant to supervise the entrant, and the care which the entrant is expected to take for his or her own safety (s.3(2)). This would include the duty say of parents or teachers to supervise children.

In *Sheehy v The Devil's Glen Tours Equestrian Centre Ltd*, High Court, Lavan J., December 10, 2001, the court applied the Occupiers' Liability Act 1995 to resolve a claim arising from a fall in the defendant's premises. The plaintiff fell and tripped over a door saddle when entering the defendant's reception area. The court, in classifying the plaintiff as a visitor, favoured the evidence of the plaintiff's engineer and found that the defendants had breached their duty to take reasonable care of the plaintiff. Lavan J. also found against the defendants on the question of contributory negligence. While the plaintiff did not look down when entering the doorway, and in fact was speaking to her daughter at the time, the court held that her behavior was not "an act of inadvertence which a reasonably careful person would not do" and did not therefore constitute contributory negligence. In *Meagher v Shamrock Public Houses Ltd (trading as the Ambassador Hotel)* [2005] I.E.H.C. 35 liability was also imposed on the defendants when the plaintiff, who had earlier paid to attend at the nightclub in the hotel, was assaulted in the defendant's carpark. Liability was imposed as the failure to have security guards patrolling that area was regarded as a breach of the "reasonable care" standard. Each case however, must be decided on the basis of its own facts.

Recreational Users

A recreational user is defined as a person who enters onto the premises of the occupier with or without the occupier's permission to engage in a recreational activity. It does not include those who have paid to enter (other than the payment of a reasonable parking charge), are members of the occupier's family who are ordinary resident on the premises, a person who has received express permission to be present, or a social guest (s.1(1)).

A recreational activity is also defined in s.1 as an activity carried out in the open air, or any scientific research or nature study conducted in the open air, or exploring caves or visiting sites and buildings of historical, architectural, traditional, artistic, archeological or scientific importance. In effect what this section does is to remove from the category of trespasser certain entrants if their purpose can be seen as having a "recreational" aspect. Its effect also could be to lower the duty owed to some, for example normally speaking coming onto the premises with implied permission of the occupier would make you a visitor and hence owed a higher duty of care. However, it now appears that if you also have a recreational purpose you will be classed as a recreational user with the corresponding lower duty.

A difficulty arises with this definition particularly with respect to those who have received an express permission to enter. It may be construed that by greeting a recreational user at the entrance to a premises might be seen as an "express invitation" thus leading the occupier into a duty to provide reasonable care.

The duty owed to recreational users is divided into two parts:

- A duty not to injure or damage the property of the entrant intentionally and the duty not to act in reckless disregard for them or their property (for reckless disregard please see below).
- A duty to take reasonable care required in the maintenance of structures which are provided primarily for the use of recreational users. This would include playgrounds, benches in parks, viewing points, stairways or gates to a national monument. This will not include gates, stiles or other structures which are not primarily used for this purpose.

As stated, the payment of an entrance fee will elevate the entrant to the status of visitor. A case that considered whether the payment of a parking fee is in effect an entrance fee was that of *Heaves v Westmeath County Council,* unreported, Circuit Court, October 17, 2001. In this case a visitor to Belvedere House slipped when descending some mossy steps. Significant in this case was that the plaintiff had paid a "car parking" fee when he arrived, but which it transpired he would have had to have paid even if he had arrived on foot, rendering it to all intents and purposes an entrance fee. This had the legal effect of elevating him to the position of visitor. Despite this no liability was found as the defendants were found to have taken reasonable care in the upkeep of the grounds and the risk which arose was an obvious one, in keeping with the character of the premises and one which had not given rise to any injuries in the past.

Trespassers

A trespasser is defined simply as a person who is not a recreational user or a visitor (s.1(1)).
  The duty owed is divided into two parts:

- A duty not to injure the entrant or damage their property intentionally and not to act with reckless disregard for them or their property (s.4(1)).
- If the entrant has a criminal intent, or commits a criminal act while on the premises the duty is simply not to injure the entrant or damage his property intentionally, there is no duty not to act with reckless disregard. This applies except where the court determines

otherwise "in the interests of justice". It is also subject to the "defence of property" principle.

If an entrant enters with permission but exceeds their right to be there and does not leave, they will become a trespasser (*Williams v Wallace Construction Ltd & Crickley Roofing Ltd and by Order, Lindab Ltd (Third Party)* [2002] 2 I.L.R.M. 62).

"To act with reckless disregard"

In determining whether an occupier has acted with reckless disregard the court will take into account the factors as outlined in s.4(2) of the Act. The factors are not determinative of liability however, and will be considered in light of the circumstances as a whole. The nine factors are:

1. Whether a danger existed the occupier knew or had reasonable grounds for believing existed on the premises.
2. Whether the occupier knew or had reasonable grounds for believing that the entrant would be present on the premises.
3. Whether the occupier knew or had reasonable grounds for believing that the entrant would be near the area of danger.
4. Whether the occupier ought reasonably to have provided protection against that danger.
5. The cost of eliminating the risk.
6. The character of the premises and the desirability of maintaining open access.
7. The conduct of the entrant.
8. The nature of any warning given, while there is no absolute duty requiring a warning, such a warning will aid the occupier in his case.
9. The expected level of supervision by others.

An examination of the concept of "reckless disregard" was carried out in the Supreme Court decision of *Weir Rodgers v The S.F. Trust Ltd* [2005] I.E.S.C. 2. The case concerned an appeal from the High Court where Butler J. had held that the landowners had acted with reckless disregard as towards the plaintiff who had fallen down a cliff at a scenic spot. The Supreme Court overturned this finding, holding that the High Court had erred in applying a standard more akin to "reasonable care" as opposed to that of "reckless disregard".

Geoghegan J. who delivered the judgment (with which Murray C.J. and Denham J. concurred) stated that:

> "For the purposes of this case and without deciding the issue, I am prepared to accept that the test of recklessness is an objective one to be interpreted as imposing a lower standard on the defendant ..."

On this basis no liability was found. It is also interesting to note that even had the standard been that of reasonable care Geoghegan J. was of the view that given the character of the area and the obvious risk posed by a cliff, no liability would have been imposed.

Modification of Duty

An occupier may, by express agreement or by notice (s.5):

- Extend his duty towards any category of entrant.
- Modify or exclude his or her duty towards visitors subject to such amendment being reasonable. If by notice the occupier must take reasonable steps to bring the notice to the attention of the visitor, such as at the normal means of access. The duty must not fall below that owed to trespassers or recreational users.

In *Hearne v Marathon Petroleum Ireland Ltd* [1998] 4 I.R. 186, the defendants sought to impose such a modification. The modification was to the effect that the defendants would take no responsibility for any loss or damage or personal injury to a visiting engineer regardless of whether it arose from their negligence or not. The court (Morris J.) found that such a modification was unreasonable and ordered that the engineer be entitled to carry out the inspection without having to sign the indemnity.

7. PRODUCTS LIABILITY

INTRODUCTION

The area of products liability concerns the right of a plaintiff to recover for damage arising from a defective product. Since the introduction of the Liability for Defective Products Act 1991 (Act) there are now two avenues which a claimant can pursue in the Irish courts. One is to prove a case in tort under the negligence principles. The other is to pursue a claim under the 1991 Act. To sue in negligence a plaintiff must show duty, breach and of course causation. The benefit of pursuing a claim under the Act is that no breach of a duty of care needs to be proved as strict liability applies (strict liability refers to liability without fault or negligence). The Act is not always the most favourable route however, certain restrictions exist in a claim taken under the Act which do not exist in an action in negligence.

ACTION IN NEGLIGENCE

Historically, there was a reluctance to allow anyone other than a customer to recover against those responsible for defective products. The classic common law stance was that of *caveat emptor* (buyer beware) coupled with a fear of blurring the lines between contract and tort by allowing consumers to sue for products outside of contract law. The judgment of Lord Abinger CB in *Winterbottom v Wright* (1842) 152 E.R. 402 is representative of this viewpoint. In that case he stated that "… unless we confine the operation of such contracts as this to the parties who enter into them, the most absurd and outrageous consequences to which I can see no limit, would ensue …". This position however, was eventually altered by the seminal decision in *Donoghue v Stevenson* [1932] A.C. 562 (see Chapter 3) where the plaintiff was allowed to recover against the manufacturer of a defective product. In this case Lord Aiken, in addition to setting out in his now famous "neighbour principle", also stated the following:

> "[A] manufacturer of products, which he sells in such a form as to show that he intends them to reach the ultimate consumer in the form in which they left him with no reasonable possibility of intermediate examination and the knowledge that

the absence of reasonable care in preparation or putting up of
the products will result in an injury to the consumer's life or
property, owes a duty to the consumer to take that reasonable
care."

In subsequent case law this duty was extended beyond that of manufacturers to cover repairers (*Power v Bedford Motor Co* [1959] I.R.
391), installers and assemblers (*Brown v Cotterill* (1938) 51 T.L.R. 21
(KBD)), suppliers (*Keegan v Owens* [1953] I.R. 267) and retailers
(*Duffy v Rooney and Dunnes Stores (Dundalk) Ltd*, High Court, June
23, 1997).

To whom is the Duty Owed?

As stated by Lord Aiken in *Donoghue v Stevenson* [1932] A.C. 562 a
duty is owed to the "the ultimate consumer." This has been held to
include anyone who uses the product, regardless of whether or not they
purchased it. In *Power v Bedford Motor Co* [1959] I.R. 391 in a case
involving a car which had been repaired by a garage for the first owner,
a duty of care was held to extend to the second owner, who tragically
was killed by the garage's negligent repair work. Lavery J. in this case
held that,

> "... the deceased did belong to that class of persons whom
> [the defendants] ought to have contemplated ... that class of
> persons included any person who might drive the car or be a
> passenger in the car and perhaps others who might be injured if
> the car went out of control ... ".

Suppliers of Component Parts

In the event that the injury arises because of a defective component
part the manufacturer may be able to pass liability to the supplier.
Whether a manufacturer can do so essentially depends on the
reasonableness of reliance on the supplier's good name. If it is a
reputable supplier and the manufacturer has taken all reasonable care
in ensuring the bona fides of the supplier's competence then it is
unlikely that the manufacturer will be liable. In *Fleming v Henry
Denny & Sons Ltd*, Supreme Court, July 29, 1955, the plaintiff sought
to recover from the defendants when he found some steel in black
pudding manufactured by them. The defendants in this case were

found not liable, in that it had been held to be reasonable for them to rely on the good name of the suppliers who supplied them with the ingredients which made up the black pudding.

Non-dangerous Defects

Once the courts overcame their initial reluctance to allow recovery in negligence for defective products there was no difficulty in compensating for dangerous defects. However, there has been greater reluctance in extending this duty to allow recovery for non-dangerous defects. The courts would happily compensate injury arising from a faulty chair leg, but would not compensate any financial loss incurred because the chair delivered to your house was the wrong colour. This stems from the general reluctance to allow recovery for "pure economic loss" (see Chapter 4) but equally from a reluctance to confuse the areas of contract and tort. The *Junior Books Ltd v Veitchi* [1983] 1 A.C. 520 decision in Britain represented a temporary change in the attitude of the English courts to such claims. In that case the defendants had installed a floor in the plaintiff's factory which was not suitable. The plaintiffs went to some expense in replacing the floor but admitted that the floor was not in any way dangerous. They sought to recover damages to compensate them for their loss. In allowing them to succeed the court stressed the reliance which the factory had on the skill of the defendants in installing suitable flooring. This case however, proved to be the exception rather than the rule and was quickly overruled by the English courts on their return to a more incremental development of incidents of duty.

Junior Books however, was followed in Ireland in the case of *Ward v McMaster* [1985] I.R. 29 where a vendor/builder sold a house which contained both dangerous and non-dangerous defects. In finding for the plaintiffs, recovery was allowed for non-dangerous defects on the basis of the principles of proximity and foreseeability. Costello J. held that the builder ought to be liable not only for dangerous defects but also for defects of quality that could cause financial loss. This decision, while supportive of a right to recover for non-dangerous defects is not however, the last word on these types of claims in Irish courts. Disapproval for such an approach has been expressed by our Supreme Court in the recent decision in *Glencar Exploration Plc v Mayo County Council* [2002] 1 I.R. 84. Keane C.J. in that case, stated that the question of whether "the decision of the House of Lords in *Junior Books Ltd v. Veitchi Co. Ltd* should be followed in this jurisdiction" was yet to be decided, demonstrating a marked reluctance to apply the principles of negligence to loss arising from non-dangerous defects. It thus remains to be seen how the Irish courts will decide such cases in the future.

ACTION IN STRICT LIABILITY: LIABILITY FOR DEFECTIVE PRODUCTS ACT 1991

The Liability for Defective Products Act 1991 (Act) was introduced to implement a European directive on products liability, Directive 85/374. Rather than replace the existing common law, the Act merely provides another avenue whereby a party may seek a remedy.

Basis for Liability

The Act provides a remedy for those who have been injured (through either physical damage to property or personal injury) by defective products in a non-commercial capacity to recover against the producer of that item. The claimant does not have to prove negligence as strict liability applies. All that must be shown is a causal connection between the product and the damage.

Product

The Act defines a product in s.1(1) as "All movables, even where the movables are incorporated into other movables or into immovables." Land and houses would generally be seen to be immovables and are thus not included in the scope of protection of the Act. However, the Act and Directive both state that where movables are incorporated into immovables and a defect arises, the producer will be liable. Thus if a house collapses there is no liability under the Act. If however, it can be shown that the house collapsed due to a defective product in the house then liability would attach (e.g. defective bricks, wood and so on).

The Act applies only to products put into circulation after the commencement of the Act i.e. post-1991. This is not in harmony with the Directive, where the date given is 1988, the year in which the Directive ought to have been implemented. This does not appear to have led to any problems in the past decade.

Primary agricultural products produced prior to December 2000 are not included in this definition, when the exception was removed due to CJD concerns (Directive 1999/34). It includes in that instance, the products of the soil, of stock-farming and of fisheries and game, excluding products which have undergone initial processing (i.e. any processing of an industrial nature).

Producer

Section 2(2) defines a "producer" as including manufacturers or producers of the product or component parts, importers of the product into the EU (if imported for commercial purposes), those who hold themselves out to be the product's producers and those in the case of agricultural products who carry out initial processing (however this will only apply to those products prior to December 2000, when the exemption for primary agricultural products was removed).

In the case where the producer of the product cannot be identified the supplier(s) of the product, usually the retailer, will be treated as the producer unless they notify the plaintiff within a reasonable time of who supplied the product to them. What constitutes a "reasonable" timeframe has not been defined.

"Defective"

A product is defective where it fails to provide the safety expected. Thus the Act clearly excludes recovery for any non-dangerous defects. It also clearly refers to safety levels which could reasonably be expected and not any absolute level of safety. In this respect, the Act states that regard must be had to:

- The presentation of the product, this includes liability for failing to warn of any possible dangers which the product might have.
- The use to which you could reasonably expect the product to be put, unreasonable use may not absolve a producer completely but rather lead to a finding of contributory negligence against the plaintiff.
- The time the product was put into circulation. This last point is to have regard to changing circumstances. A product must be judged in the light of standards prevailing at the time it was issued. A product also must be judged in light of how long it could reasonably be expected to last. If you buy vegetables for instance it is not reasonable that they be edible after a number of weeks, however a car would be expected to last without incident for a number of years.

The emphasis here is on safety and not simply on the product falling below what a consumer might expect unlike the situation which can arise in negligence under tort, where a plaintiff could recover for damage or injury suffered due to a non-dangerous product. In the English decision of *Abouzaid v Mothercare Ltd*, unreported, December 21, 2000, a strap on a sleeping bag attachment for a baby's pushchair which comprised of an elasticated band with a metal buckle at the end, was found to have a defective design. The band had sprung back, hitting a boy in the eye as he attempted to fasten the sleeping-bag to his baby brother's pushchair. In *A v National Blood Authority* [2001] 3 All E.R. 289 a woman who had contracted Hepatitis C from contaminated blood products took a case against the defendants arguing that the blood was defective. The defendants tried to argue that as the public was not entitled to expect safe blood it was not defective with respect to the Act. The court (Burton J.) rejected this argument, stating that the public was entitled to expect blood products free from contamination. There had been no warnings, and no publicity to inform the public otherwise.

Damage

Damage is defined in s.1 as:

(a) Death or personal injury, or
(b) Loss of, damage to, or destruction of any item or property other than the defective product itself;

Provided that the item of property:

 (i) is of a type ordinarily intended for private use or consumption and
(ii) was used by the injured person mainly for his own private use or consumption.

"Personal injury" is further defined in s.1 to include "any disease and any impairment of a person's physical or mental condition". This appears to cover pain and suffering and conditions such as nervous shock.

Note also that the damage suffered must be personal or if physical, to something other than the product itself. Destruction of the product alone will not give rise to an action under the Act.

Limitations

In Damage

Section 3 states that property damage must exceed £350 (€445 approximately) before recovery is allowed. Where damage exceeds that amount only that amount in excess of the minimum is recoverable. The purpose of such a limitation is to limit spurious claims. There is no limit for personal injury actions.

In Time

Section 7 states that the right of action expires three years from the date on which the cause of action accrued or the date, if later, on which the plaintiff became aware or should reasonably have become aware of the damage, the defect and the identity of the producer. All rights of action expire after a 10 year period from the date on which the product in question was put into circulation. If judicial proceedings are however pending, or have started at the end of the 10 year period then they may continue.

Who Can Recover

Any person who has suffered injury as a result of a defective product, or in the event of that person's death, his or her representative, can sue under the Act.

Defences

Section 6 of the Act list a number of defences on which a producer can rely:

1. That she or he did not put the product into circulation. Circulation is defined as when a product is delivered to another person in the course of business or when it is incorporated into another movable product.

In the Danish case of Case C-203/99 *Veedfald v Arhus Amtskommune* [2001] E.C.R. I-3569, the European Court of Justice (ECJ) considered whether defective fluid used to wash a kidney prior to an organ transplant, had been put into circulation given that the procedure was a medical one paid for by the State. The ECJ ruled that notwithstanding the medical and public nature of the procedure that the manufacturers had circulated the fluid in a commercial capacity and it fell within the provisions of the Directive.

2. That having regard to the circumstances it is probable that the defect which caused the damage did not exist at the time the product was put into circulation by him or that this defect came into being afterwards. Needless to say this can be extremely difficult to prove.
3. That the product was not manufactured by him/her for sale or any form of distribution for an economic purpose nor manufactured or distributed by him/her in the course of his business. Essentially this means that the Act will not apply to private transactions.
4. That the defect is due to compliance with an EC standard or law.
5. That the state of scientific knowledge at the time when s/he put the product into circulation was not such as to enable the existence of the defect to be discovered (development risks defence).

In *Commission v UK* [1997] All E.R. (EC) 481 the ECJ offered the following clarification on the meaning of "scientific knowledge":

a. Article 7(e) refers not only to the state of scientific and technical knowledge of the industrial sector, but that in the world at large at the time the product was put into circulation.
b. This knowledge must have been accessible to the producer at the time the product was put into circulation.

6. In the case of the manufacturer of a component or the producer of a raw material, the defect is attributable entirely to the design of the product in which the component has been fitted or the raw material has been incorporated or to the instructions given by the manufacturer of the product.

8. EMPLOYERS' LIABILITY

INTRODUCTION

Employers' liability deals with the liability of employers for occupational injuries to employees arising from an employer's negligence. Initially there was very little protection for employees within the workplace with respect to their health and safety. Employers could also avail of defences such as the defence common employment and voluntary assumption of risk to defeat a claim. This has largely changed and in addition to a raft of legislation imposing workplace health and safety standards (in particular the General Applications Regulations 2007) the tort of negligence has developed to provide employees with a remedy.

An action may now be brought by injured employees in negligence, for a breach of protective legislation or by invoking the principle of vicarious liability. Vicarious liability also imposes liability on an employer for the negligent action of an employee under his or her control even if the employer himself or herself has not acted negligently (see Chapter 9).

This chapter will deal primarily with the action in negligence.

STANDARD

The standard imposed in negligence, as we might recall from Chapter 3, is that of reasonable care. Similarly in employment cases, the principle as stated in *Bradley v CIE* [1976] I.R. 217 by Henchy J. is that: "The law does not require an employer to ensure in all circumstances the safety of his workmen. He will have discharged his duty if he has done what a reasonable and prudent employer would have done in the circumstances."

The mere existence of an injury will not be enough to show liability, the plaintiff must show that that the injury was foreseeable and as result of the defendant failing to take reasonable care. In *Brady v Beckmann Instruments (Galway) Inc* [1986] I.L.R.M. 361 the plaintiff, an employee of the defendants, had contracted a form of dermatitis by inhaling chemical fumes at his workplace. The evidence showed that the standard at the plant was superior to that found in most plants of its kind and as the likelihood of injury was "so unique and improbable as not to have been reasonably foreseeable by his employers" no liability was imposed.

DUTIES

The duty of the employer to the employee can be discussed in relation to four principal duties, although there is a considerable degree of overlap. They are the:

* Duty to provide competent staff;
* Duty to provide a safe place of work;
* Duty to provide a safe system of work;
* Duty to provide proper equipment.

Competent Staff

An employer is under a duty to use due care to select proper and competent staff. As stated in *Skerritt v Scallan* (1877) I.R. 11: "The duty which a master owes his servant is to use due care to select proper and competent fellow servants". An employer is also under a duty to ensure that employees have been adequately instructed in the operation of any tools or equipment and in the carrying out of their jobs.

In *Hough v Irish Base Metals Ltd*, unreported, Supreme Court, December 8, 1967, liability was not imposed on an employer when an employee was injured by another employee who had pushed him onto a gas fire. In finding the employers not liable the court held that "the larking in question was of such recent origin and was not of such frequency as must necessarily have been detected in any system of reasonable supervision". On the other hand, in *Hudson v Ridge Manufacturing* [1957] 2 Q.B. 348 liability was imposed where an employee was injured by a second employee who tripped him. As stated by Streatfield J. there existed a danger "through the conduct of one of the defendants' employees, of which they knew, repeated conduct which went on over a long period of time, and which they did nothing whatever to remove".

Safe Place of Work

The employer is obliged to supply a safe place of work. In cases where an unsafe place of work exists it will be no defence for the employer to state that the employee knew of the dangers inherent in the workplace.

The duty is not as absolute one. As stated by Kingsmill Moore J. in *Christie v Odean (Ireland Ltd)* (1957) 91 I.L.T.R. 25 "to make accidents impossible would often be to make work impossible".

The concept of workplace includes all places where the employee works including places away from the main place of work. In *Mulcare v Southern Health Board* [1988] I.L.R.M. 689, a home help employed by the defendants hurt her ankle on an uneven floor in the dilapidated house of an elderly woman whom she had visited for several years. She argued that the defendants were negligent in not having surveyed the house. In this case it was held that the house was not really unsafe and that the onus was not on the Health Board to carry out an examination of every premises their home help worked in. Central to the court's decision was the high social utility of visiting the elderly in their homes coupled with the low probability of such an accident occurring.

Worthy of note is that an employer also owes a duty to those employees who work from home. A Code of Practice on e-working was published by the Department of Enterprise in 2000 which gives guidance to employers on how to protect their employees' safety in these cases.

Proper Equipment

An employer is under a duty to take reasonable care to ensure that proper appliances are provided and maintained in a proper condition so as not to subject those employed to unnecessary risk and to provide such personal protective equipment or clothing as is necessary for the employee to carry out duties safely.

Inaction by the employer where he or she has been notified of a defective piece of equipment will almost certainly lead to liability as in *Burke v John Paul & Co Ltd* [1967] I.R. 277 where liability was imposed on an employer for allowing the employee to use a blunt cutting instrument.

If reasonable steps are taken by the employer to address risks to safety, no liability will be found. In *Rogers v Bus Átha Cliath*, unreported, Circuit Court, January 17, 2000 for instance, no liability was found when a bus driver was injured in an attack. In reaching his decision McMahon J. pointed to the significant investment made by the defendants in identifying suitable protective screens which were being installed on a gradual basis on all buses. In a factually similar case a number of years later however, *Corkery v Bus Éireann,* (unreported, Supreme Court, Keane C.J., May 6, 2003) liability was imposed. Unlike the *Rogers* case, the defendants maintained that the risk to safety did not warrant a screen to be installed. The High Court and on appeal the Supreme Court rejected this claim, given the very low cost of the screens (€500) and the evidence that in Dublin and other cities crime was on the increase rendering such protective screens necessary.

Safe System of Work

An employer is under a duty to provide a safe system of work. Central to this requirement is the responsibility of an employer to provide training in the carrying out of duties and to repeat such training at regular intervals. In *Barclay v An Post* [1998] 2 I.L.R.M. 285 however, provision of training was found not to be enough when an employer allowed an employee to expose himself to risk of injury. Barclay, a postman, had returned to work following a bank injury and undertook voluntary overtime on an estate with low lying letter boxes, which led him to suffer a second back injury. Notwithstanding the training offered in manual handling, liability was imposed by McGuinness J. who stated that "the defendant's duty of care toward the plaintiff included a duty to ensure that, in the short term after his illness, he did not take up duties which would put undue and extraordinary strain on his back".

DANGEROUS WORK SITUATIONS

While the courts will accept greater risks in particular work situations, such as the defence forces and security guards, it will not absolve an employer of liability in all cases. As highlighted in *Ryan v Ireland* [1989] I.R. 177 the duty of the employer is to reduce the risk as far as is reasonably possible. In this case the plaintiff was serving as a soldier in the Lebanon. While on guard duty at a guard post he was subjected to an attack and injured. While the plaintiff accepted that he was engaged in a dangerous work situation where injury was likely he argued that the guard post had been inadequately sandbagged. The court agreed, imposing liability on the defendants for failing to minimize the risk. Similarly in *Walsh v Securicor (Ireland) Ltd* [1993] 2 I.R. 507 liability was imposed when the plaintiff was injured in a robbery on a security van. In this case the defendants were criticized for failing to adequately investigate methods by which risks to security personnel could be reduced.

PSYCHIATRIC INJURY

It is undisputed that an employee may recover damages not only for physical injury but also for psychiatric injury that arises due to the negligence of an employer. In this regard s.2 of the Civil Liability Act 1961 provides that "'Personal Injury' includes any disease and any impairment of a person's physical or mental condition and 'injured' shall be construed accordingly."

In the case of nervous shock clear guidelines have been provided in a number of cases including that of *Curran v Cadbury* [2000] 2 I.L.R.M. 343 (see Chapter 5). Outside of the realm of "nervous shock", which is limited by the confines of that tort, employees may suffer psychiatric injury from being bullied in the workplace, by being overworked, or by being exposed to dangers to their health. In these cases the application of tort principles to psychiatric injury has proved more troublesome.

Bullying

Bullying has been defined by the Health and Safety Authority (HSA) as "repeated inappropriate behaviour, direct or indirect, whether verbal, physical or otherwise, conducted by one or more persons against another or others, at the place of work and/or in the course of employment, which could reasonably be regarded as undermining the individual's right to dignity at work".

If allowed to continue in the workplace it can be seen as a breach both of the common law duty of care and of legislation. Sections 8(2)(b) and 13(1)(e) of the Safety, Health and Welfare at Work Act 2005 place obligations on employers to protect employees' safety at work which the HSA has interpreted as including an obligation to protect against workplace bullying. In *Saehan Media Ireland Ltd v A Worker* [1999] E.L.R. 41 the Labour Court awarded compensation due to the fact that no grievance procedure was in place to deal with the alleged bullying.

However, very few cases have come before the courts claiming damages for bullying behaviour. This is largely due to the difficulty of bringing a case of bullying and the inevitable reluctance of a victim of bullying to expose themselves to the rigours of a court trial. The majority of bullying cases which have come before legal bodies are those cases taken as "constructive dismissal" cases, under the Unfair Dismissals Act 1977–2005. Constructive dismissal is when an employee is forced to leave the workplace due to that workplace becoming intolerable. A case of this kind was the widely publicized case of Liz Allen, the former crime writer with the Sunday Independent, who brought a claim of bullying resulting in constructive dismissal against her employers—*Allen v Independent Newspapers* [2002] 13 E.L.R. 84.

The difficulty of succeeding in a bullying action was clearly evident in the Supreme Court decision *Quigley v Complex Tooling and Moulding Ltd* [2008] I.E.S.C. 44. In this case, despite there being clear evidence of bullying the Supreme Court overturned the High Court finding in the plaintiff's favour on the basis that insufficient evidence had been presented to show that the bullying was causatively responsible for the plaintiff's mental injuries.

In drawing up a policy on bullying employers can look to the Code of Practice for Employers and Employees on Prevention and Resolution of Bullying at Work 2007 (Health and Safety Authority) for guidance.

Stress from Overwork

The vast majority of psychiatric cases taken involve an employee who has suffered from a nervous breakdown or other mental disease as a result of being overworked.

The most significant High Court decision in recent years is that of *McGrath v Trintech Technologies Ltd* [2005] 4 I.R. 382. In this case Laffoy J. in the High Court affirmed the "16 practical propositions" laid down by Hale L.J. in the English case of *Sutherland v Hatton* [2002] EWCA Civ 7. These held that liability was to be decided on the basis of ordinary negligence principles. No workplace should be considered "inherently dangerous", instead foreseeability of injury would be decided on the basis of what the employer knows. This in turn depended on the character of the individual employee and on his/her representations (including presentation of medical evidence) to the employer, an employer is not required to make searching inquiries but rather is entitled to take what the employee says at face value. In each case, even in cases of foreseeable injury, an employer would only be entitled to do what was reasonable in the circumstances, based on available resources and other considerations. In the event that demotion or dismissal were the only available options the employer did not have to act, it would fall to the employee to remove themselves from the job before irreparable damage was done. Finally, causation would have to be proven in all cases, it was open for a court to find that the cause of the injury was not the workplace, but some other factor outside of the employment situation. In the *Sutherland* case, of the four appeals taken by the employers against trial court findings, three were successful. A further successful appeal by one of these three was taken to the House of Lords—*Barber v Somerset County Council* [2004] UKHL 14. In the *McGrath* case, no liability was found as the plaintiff had failed to prove that the mental injury to him was foreseeable. In addition, he had failed to show that the injury was caused by any breach of the General Applications Regulations (which had formed a further basis to his claim). Following from McGrath, the decision in *Maher v Jabil* [2005] 16 E.L.R. 233 distilled the principles above to the following three questions (later applied in *Berber v Dunnes Stores* [2009] I.E.S.C. 10):

1. Had the plaintiff suffered an injury to health?
2. Was it caused by the workplace?
3. Was it foreseeable?

The plaintiff in that case had initially complained of suffering stress as a result of being overworked and when on his return to work he was demoted to a less stressful job he suffered stress from being in a less challenging role. However, the court (Clarke J.) found that foreseeability of injury had not been established. As the plaintiff's workload had initially been comparable to that of other employees no foreseeability was found in relation to his first injury, and as his second workload was lower, no foreseeability was found to have arisen from this injury either.

Exposure to Danger/Fear of Disease/Worried-well Cases

Recent case law has emerged in the courts involving employees who have developed a mental injury from the anxiety of having been negligently exposed to a substance that may cause injury in the future. These have been referred to as the "worried-well" cases. The most celebrated of these cases is that of *Fletcher v Commissioners of Public Works* [2003] 2 I.L.R.M. 94. In this case the plaintiff had developed a reactive anxiety neurosis as a result of being negligently exposed to asbestos when working as a general operative in Leinster House between 1985 and 1991. Although the dangers of such exposure were well known to the employer nothing was done to protect the employee. He subsequently learned of the exposure and become acutely worried that he would develop one or more of the severe illnesses that could arise despite there being no physical evidence to support his concerns. The plaintiff succeeded in the High Court but this was appealed to the Supreme Court. The defendants accepted that they had acted negligently but argued that the injury suffered by the plaintiff was not foreseeable. Keane C.J. agreed holding that Fletcher had to fall into one of two categories to succeed—that of nervous shock or that of negligence. He held that this was not a nervous shock case. As for a negligence action Keane C.J. stated that there might be liability where the plaintiff suffered a combination of anger and anxiety, foreseeable to a person of "ordinary fortitude". However, in a highly unsympathetic judgment, Keane C.J. ultimately held that liability should not be imposed. Included in his "policy reasons" for rejecting liability, he included the following:

- Firstly the undesirability of awarding damages to plaintiffs who have suffered no physical injury and whose psychiatric condition is solely due to an unfounded fear of contracting a particular disease.
- Secondly the implications for the health care field of a more relaxed rule as to recovery for psychiatric illness.

DEFENCES

Contributory Negligence

An employer's liability may be limited to the extent that the employee contributed to the accident or fault. Awareness of a danger will not necessarily constitute contributory negligence as the courts accept that the primary responsibility rests on the employer to both correct dangerous practices and ensure that they don't develop. This is particularly the case in relation to inexperienced new employees. As stated in *McKenna v Meighan* [1966] I.R. 288 by Walsh J.: "It is well established that the workman's knowledge of the danger is not in itself contributory negligence ..."

The court will only impose liability on the plaintiff where the plaintiff has acted unreasonably in the circumstances. In *Allen v Ó Súilleabhán* High Court, Kinlen J., July 28, 1995, a 25-year-old student midwife sustained a serious back injury when holding the leg of a woman who was giving birth. Although aware at the time of the strain which she was subjecting herself to no liability attached to her from her actions as it was felt that it would have been extremely difficult for a student midwife to interrupt or complain during the procedure.

Every worker however, is required to have regard for their own safety. In *O'Reilly v Iarnród Éireann* [2002] 6 I.C.L.M.D. 119 the plaintiff was injured when he stepped off a train that was traveling at between five and 15 mph. The employer was held liable as it was a long-standing tradition that had not been corrected but the employee was also found 25 per cent contributory negligent for failing to have taken due regard for his own safety.

In some cases where the actions of the employee were due to failure of an employer to correct a bad practice then the employee will not be liable. In *Stewart v Killeen Paper Mills Ltd* [1959] I.R. 436, an employer routinely left a machine unguarded causing an employee to take a chance in removing paper from it, resulting in injury to the employee. In the Supreme Court on the issue of contributory negligence Kingsmill-Moore J. stated that: "Where it can be shown that a regular practice exists unchecked it is difficult to convict of contributory negligence a workman who follows such practice."

Voluntary Assumption of Risk

The principle of *volenti non fit injuria* holds that if an employee undertakes employment which might be a risk to his health and safety then they cannot expect to claim once something goes wrong. Although this principle had featured in the earlier common law it is of less relevance today. In particular its effectiveness has been severely curtailed by s.34 of the Civil Liability Act 1961, which makes clear that the defence of *volenti non fit injuria* will not prevail without a clear, communicated waiver by the employee to the effect that they will not hold an employer to count where an injury occurs.

Defence of Common Employment

This defence simply put meant that if an employee were injured due to the behaviour of fellow employees then no liability would attach to the employer regardless of the circumstances of the injury. The inherent unfairness of this doctrine led to it being completely overturned by the Law Reform (Personal Injuries) Act 1958. Section 1(2) of this Act states that it will no longer be a defence for an employer to claim as a defence that the person injured was in "common employment" with the person who injured him.

9. VICARIOUS LIABILITY

INTRODUCTION

Vicarious liability refers to the liability of one person for the actions of another although that person is free from any personal blameworthiness or fault. As such it constitutes an example of strict or no-fault liability. The person for whom the defendant is said to be vicariously liable must have acted negligent for vicarious liability to arise. Earliest examples included the liability of a husband for the torts of his wife and the liability of a master for the actions of his or her servants. In the former case, this reflected the earlier position where a man owned his wife's property on marriage, after the property acts of the 1880s however the principle of vicarious liability within marriage gradually disappeared. In respect of the master/servant relationship, it was modified to the extent that the wrongdoing had to take place within the course of the employee's employment. It was largely held that an employer should take responsibility for his employee's wrongdoing as this would encourage employers to take greater care in disciplining employees. It also meant that an employer, who might be more financially secure, would absorb the cost of any litigation. Vicarious liability also arises in the cases of partners in firms and in relation to car ownership.

CONTROL

Before a defendant can be held vicariously liable they must have been in a position of control over the wrongdoer. This extends to any given situation including that of guests in a person's home as in the case of *Moynihan v Moynihan* [1975] I.R. 192. In this case the plaintiff, the granddaughter of the defendant, had been scalded by a pot of tea prepared by the defendant's daughter and left unattended. In finding the grandmother vicariously liable the court focused on the role of the grandmother as a controller of the guests in her house, and in particular in the serving of refreshments. Walsh J. stated that "on the evidence ... the necessary element of control was vested in the defendant and the daughter Marie was in the de facto service of her mother for the purpose of the act in which she was alleged to be negligent." However, this has most recently been described as somewhat of a high watermark for vicarious liability and it is unclear whether the courts would find the same way today. In the most recent case of significance in the area of vicarious liability, that of *O'Keeffe v Hickey* [2008] I.E.S.C. 72 Hardiman J. criticised the finding in Moynihan stating:

> "The case appears to me to be an early example of the dismantling or muddying of the long established boundaries or limits of vicarious liability. This was done for the very humane reason of helping an innocent injured party to recover compensation, but it was done at a very considerable social cost, not often considered or discussed ..."

In *O'Keeffe* the plaintiff had taken an action against the State arguing that it was vicariously liable for abuse which took place when she attended national school in the early 1970s. The Supreme Court found that the State did not exercise the necessary degree of control over the teacher who carried out the abuse, given that that person was appointed and managed by a Board of Management and not by the State.

VICARIOUS LIABILITY OF EMPLOYERS

An employer can be held vicariously liable for the negligent acts of employees carried out in the course of their employment. Vicarious liability differs from strict employer's liability in that in employer's liability the employer himself is responsible for some wrongdoing while for vicarious liability no wrongdoing on the part of the employer is necessary. In the discussion of when an employer becomes vicariously liable for the actions of employees a number of issues are relevant:

- Who is the employer?
- Who is the employee?
- Can there ever be liability for the actions of an independent contractor?
- When is an employee acting in the "course of employment"?

Who is the Employer?

In an action for the vicarious liability of an employer it is important that the correct employer is pursued. While this appears self-evident confusion can arise, particularly in the case of hired employees who negligently injure their colleagues. Where an employee is hired out a question arises as to whether the temporary employer or the original employer is the true employer for the purposes of an action. The answer will generally be that the employee remains the employee of the first employer. This is based on the principle of control, it is assumed that the hired employee is hired because of some special skill or expertise and as such the temporary employer does not have a say in how the work is done, that is to say that the temporary employer does not have a sufficient degree of control.

In *Lynch v Palgrave Murphy Ltd* [1964] I.R. 150 a forklift operator was hired by the defendants from Crosbie. The forklift operator (Byrne) injured another employee who then sought to recover from the defendants for the negligence of Byrne. In finding the defendants not liable the court held that a sufficient degree of control had not passed from Crosbie to the defendants. While the defendants did direct Byrne generally as to how to do the job, he was still employed, paid and subject to dismissal by Crosbie. On the other hand sufficient control was deemed to have passed in the case of *McDonagh v O'Connell*, unreported, High Court, Barr J., October 24, 1996. In this case a labourer who worked for a contractor was on loan to Limerick Corporation for some archaeological work. He did not have any specialised knowledge in the area himself and worked under the supervision of the Corporation's archaeologists. He was injured when a trench collapsed on him. In finding the Corporation liable they held that in this case, and due to the specialised nature of the work, the Corporation was the proper defendant as it was the employer who controlled how the work was carried out. As held by the court:

"In ordinary course, the determining factor in deciding whether or not the original employer is liable in negligence to a worker he has loaned to another, in connection with injuries sustained in course of such work, turns upon the direction and control of the worker at the material time."

Who is the Employee?

Before an injured employee can sue the employer for vicarious liability the person who caused the injury must also be an employee under the employer's control. In most cases this will be the case, but in others the worker may not be an employee but rather an independent contractor.

An independent contractor is said to work under a contract for services, and works essentially for himself. Traditionally they are paid a lump sum, work for a limited period or for a limited project, and deal with their own taxes. Examples of independent contractors include plumbers, solicitors, and other workers who are essentially self-employed. An employer although hiring an independent contractor for a specific job, will not be seen to be vicariously liable for the wrong-doing of such a worker. On the other hand an employee is said to work under a contract of services, they are generally hired on an ongoing basis, work under the direction of the employer and do not deal with their own tax affairs. An employer may be liable for the actions of an employee. The thorny issue of determining who constitutes an employee and is not an independent contractor has been a difficult one for the courts. There is no straightforward way of reaching a conclusion, as stated by Barr J. in *McAuliffe v Minister for Social Welfare* [1995] 2 I.R. 238 "it is not possible to devise any hard and fast rule as to what constitutes a servant and what constitutes an independent contractor. Each case must be considered on its own special facts in the light of the broad guidelines which caselaw provides."

In general the courts will look at issues of control, the degree of integration of the worker into the workplace, whether the worker works for himself or for the employer and the terms of the contract. None of these elements is in itself decisive but must all be considered before a decision can be reached.

Acting in the "course of employment"

An employer will only be held liable for the negligent acts of his or her employees where the employee has been acting in the course of his or her employment. The precise meaning to be given to "course of employment" has differed over the years but in general it is held that if the employee is doing what they have been employed to do, regardless of how well or badly they are doing it, the employer will be held liable.

In *Farry v GN Rly Co* [1898] 2 I.R. a station employee negligently detained the plaintiff to force him to give up his ticket. The company ultimately were held responsible for false imprisonment, as although the employee was wrong to detain the plaintiff as he did, he clearly was doing it in the belief that it was part of his job. However, where the employee is doing something which they have not been employed to do, no liability will attach. This applied in the case of *Irving & Irving v Post Office* [1987] I.R.L.R. 289, where a postman-sorter who wrote on offensive racist remark on a letter destined for a couple of Jamaican origin, was not deemed to be acting in the "course of his employment."

More recently, the courts in England (*Lister v Hesley Hall Ltd* [2002] 1 A.C. 215) have developed a "close connection" test in deciding whether an employee is acting in the course of his employment. On the basis of this test an act can be within the course of employment if the nature of the employment itself allows for the act to take place. In the *Lister* case, sexual abuse was held to have occurred within the "course of employment" as the nature of the employment gave rise to the necessary degree of power and intimacy for such an act to occur. This view appears to have found favour in an Irish sexual abuse case, that of *Delahunty v South Eastern Health Board* [2003] I.E.H.C. 132. In that case O'Higgins J. referred to the fact that there was not a sufficiently "strong connection" between the parties as the victim was a visitor to the institution where he was assaulted. It was argued in that case that to apply Lister would involve a "departure in the law", a question which O'Higgins J. stated would await a "fuller analysis of the judgement". In the recent case of *O'Keeffe v Hickey* [2008] I.E.S.C. 72 discussed above, as liability of the State was rejected on the basis of lack of requisite control the issue of whether the act came within the scope of employment was not fully addressed. However, Hardiman J. was clearly of the view that the "close connection" test should be rejected by the Irish courts, with Fennelly J. lending it some support. The current position is that without a definitive statement it remains to be seen as to whether it will be fully adopted by the Irish courts.

An employee is not acting in the course of employment while on the way to or from work but any trips taken in connection with work once there will be deemed to be within the course of employment. A question arises however, as to how far from a determined route an employee is allowed to venture before acting outside the course of employment. A number of cases have been helpful in this regard. The rule appears to be that slight deviations will not constitute a detour capable of taking an employee outside the "course of employment" whereas a major departure will. A comparison between *O'Connell v Bateman* [1932] L.J. Ir. 160 with *Jameson v Byrne and Maguire* (1926) 60 I.L.T.R. 11 is illustrative of this point. In the former case, an employee borrowed his employer's lorry after work to visit his parents. An accident resulted but the employers were found not to be vicariously liable as the taking of the car was for a purpose completely unrelated to work. On the other hand, in *Jameson*, an employee who while on a return trip from a petrol delivery made a detour and was involved in an accident, was found to be acting within the course of his employment.

LIABILITY OF A FIRM FOR A PARTNER'S WRONGS

Partners in a firm may also be vicariously liable for each others negligent acts. This liability is very similar to that of an employer for the torts of their employee. A partner must be held to be working within the course of his or her employment before liability will attach to the firm.

Sections 9 and 11 of the Partnership Act 1890 also state that "where acting in the ordinary course of the business of the firm or with the authority of his co-partners, loss or injury is caused to any person not being a partner in the firm … the firm is liable therefore to the same extent as the partner so acting or omitting to act."

LIABILITY OF OWNERS OF CARS

Owners of cars can also be liable for any injury which arises because of a misuse of their car by another. Liability in this area is governed by the Road Traffic Act 1961. Section 118 of this Act states that, "Where a person uses a mechanically propelled vehicle with the consent of the owner of the vehicle the user shall for the purpose of determining liability … be deemed to use the vehicle as the employee of the owner …"

Before liability attaches under this section the consent given to use the car must be real. In *Kelly v Lombard Motor Co Ltd* [1974] I.R. 142 for instance the defendants were a car hire company who had hired a car to Patrick O'Donnell who used the driving licence of a friend to secure the car. Here the court held that consent was not given to O'Donnell but to his friend and therefore the car hire company were not liable for the injury that arose. Likewise if consent is given for a particular purpose, then this consent must not be exceeded or the consent will not longer constitute good consent.

An owner of a car may also be liable for the negligent acts of passengers travelling in the car where it would be reasonable for the owner of the car to control their actions. This would arise particularly in the case of child passengers but also in the case of passengers who are incapacitated in some way. In *Curley v Mannion* [1965] I.R. 543

the defendant was found to be at fault for failing to adequately supervise his 13 year old daughter who opened the car door knocking the plaintiff off her bicycle. Liability arose from the position of the defendant as owner of the car and also as the child's father.

LIABILITY FOR MEMBERS OF ONE'S FAMILY

The liability for members of one's family is a very limited liability as generally the courts are reluctant to find members of a family liable for the acts of another. Again the crucial issue is that of control. Generally speaking parents will not be liable for the torts of their children but there are two exceptions. One is where they are acting as employees of their parents, and as such vicarious liability becomes an issue. The other is where parents have failed to exercise sufficient control over their children. However, courts do not expect that parents should be with their children at all times. Regard must be had to the age of the child, the parents' knowledge of the personality and character of their children, and the reasonable freedom which children should enjoy as part of growing up.

10. MEDICAL NEGLIGENCE

INTRODUCTION

A medical practitioner can be found liable for medical negligence in two ways—by failing to take the standard of care required of a medical practitioner and/or by failing to obtain informed consent.

In the first scenario, the standard of care required by a medical practitioner in diagnosis and treatment is that described by the *Dunne* principles.

In the second scenario a practitioner may have behaved reasonably and without negligence but have failed to properly inform the patient of the treatment to be undertaken, so that the patient has not fully consented to the procedure. Failure to obtain "informed consent" will also lead to liability for medical negligence.

STANDARD

The courts do not apply strict negligence principles to medical negligence cases. Instead the standard has been tailored to reflect the fact that medical opinion often differs as to the correct course of action. To allow medical practices to develop it is also necessary to allow practitioners an element of freedom without the threat of legal action being taken against them. On the other hand doctors cannot act completely unfettered by the standards of due skill and care. To balance these conflicting concerns the law has developed a standard for the medical profession which takes account of existing practices within that profession.

The standard is that laid down in the case of *Dunne v National Maternity Hospital and Reginald Jackson* [1989] I.R. 91 where Finlay C.J. stated that in order to ascertain whether a practitioner has behaved reasonably the court must consider the following:

1. Has the medical practitioner been proved guilty of failure as no medical practitioner of equal specialist or general status and skill would be guilty of if acting with reasonable care?
2. Deviating from a general and approved practice will not constitute negligence unless the course taken would not be one taken by a like practitioner acting with reasonable care.

3. Following a general and approved practice will not constitute reasonable care if the practice in question has *inherent defects* which ought to be obvious to any person giving the matter due consideration.

See also *O'Donovan v Cork County Council* [1967] I.R. 173 (SC), where Walsh J. stated that "Neglect of duty does not cease by repetition of neglect of duty."

4. An honest difference of opinion between doctors as to which is the better of two ways of treating a patient will not constitute negligence.
5. With respect to two alternative courses of treatment all that is required is that the conduct chosen complies with the reasonable care standard, not that it was necessarily the better option.

In the *Dunne* case, which involved the delivery of twins, questions arose as to whether the monitoring of only one heartbeat during delivery satisfied the standard of reasonable care and whether a monitor ought to have been placed on the unborn baby at an earlier stage. One of the twins was born with severe brain damage and the other was delivered dead. The plaintiffs argued that had both heartbeats been monitored and the monitor applied earlier distress might have been detected at an earlier stage. Medical evidence at trial differed as to whether the injury could have been avoided by the earlier use of the monitor. It also differed as to whether two heartbeats ought to have been monitored, what was clear was that the practice of monitoring only one heartbeat was accepted practice by some practitioners. The Supreme Court in applying the principles stated above found that the hospital had followed a "general and approved practice" which was not shown to have any "inherent defects". On that basis they found no liability on the part of the hospital or consultant.

What constitutes a "general and approved practice"?

To constitute a general and approved practice the practice need not be universal, but it must be approved of and adhered to by a number of reputable practitioners holding the relevant specialist or general qualifications. They must have taken consideration of any risks attached to the practice before adopting it and reliance on it must be reasonable.

In *Bolitho v City and Hackney Health Authority* [1997] 4 All E.R.
771 the House of Lords in approving the earlier *Bolam* test stated that:

> "... the judge before accepting a body of opinion as being
> responsible, reasonable or respectable, will need to be satisfied
> that, in forming their views, the experts have directed their
> minds to the question of comparative risks and benefits and
> have reached a defensible conclusion on the matter."

In this case Lord Browne-Wilkinson also stated that:

> "... despite a body of professional opinion sanctioning the
> defendant's conduct, the defendant can properly be held liable
> for negligence ... because, in some cases, it cannot be
> demonstrated to a judge's satisfaction that the body of opinion
> relied on is reasonable or responsible."

"Honest difference of opinion between doctors"

In *Griffin v Patton* [2004] I.E.S.C. 46, Geoghegan J., in a unanimous
judgement, held that an "honest difference of opinion" related to the
method of diagnosis and treatment and not to the issue of negligence.
In this case the court approved a High Court (Donovan J.) finding that
the defendant had been negligent in leaving behind a piece of bone
when evacuating a deceased foetus, notwithstanding that some medical
experts had testified that this might have occurred without negligence. As
stated by Geoghegan J.: "The learned trial judge was perfectly entitled if
the evidence supported it, to form a view that the Respondent did not
carry out the evacuation process properly there being no disagreement
between the experts as to how such process should be done."

INNOVATIVE IDEAS/TREATMENT

Medical professionals are entitled to try innovative treatments and
procedures. A question arises however, as to when professionals can
depart from an existing practice and adopt a new one. The advice of
the courts on this matter has been largely conservative. As stated in
Crawford v Board of Governors of Charing Cross Hospital, The Times,
December 8, 1953, "The time may come in a particular case when a
new recommendation may be so well proved and so well known and
so well accepted that it should be adopted ...".

As for experimental type treatments, while it is accepted that doctors should not be free to experiment freely, once the informed consent of a patient is received then any treatment may be legitimate. It is in the situations where informed consent may be impossible to achieve (say where a person is unconscious or mentally incapacitated) that a medical practitioner ought to be very reluctant in embarking on anything other than a generally recognised and accepted practice.

CATEGORIES OF PRACTITIONERS

The standard of care expected depends to a large degree on the expertise that that professional holds themselves up as possessing.

In the case of specialists the duty was enunciated in case of *O'Donovan v Cork County Council* [1967] I.R. 173 as follows, "A medical practitioner who holds himself out as being a specialist in a particular field is required to attain the ordinary level of skill amongst those who specialise in the same field".

General practitioners (GPs) tend not to be the most commonly litigated against category of practitioners, partially no doubt due to the close relationship which GPs enjoy with their patients. GPs however, because of this close relationship are also expected to have special knowledge of patients which ought to alert them to difficulties which might not be clearly raised by the patient. In the case of *Collins v Mid Western Health Board* [2002] 2 I.R. 154 a GP was found liable for failing to adequately question the plaintiff's husband, who died from a brain hemorrhage. The GP had diagnosed a chest infection. Liability has also arisen where a GP has failed to respond to a call-out. In *O'Doherty v Whelan* (unreported, High Court, O'Hanlon J., January 18, 1993) O'Hanlon J. in finding a GP liable for failing to come to the home of a pregnant woman who had suffered two miscarriages in the past, stated:

> "That is not to say that an obligation can arise in every case where a request is made to a general practitioner to visit the patient at home, to comply with such a request. That would be wholly unreasonable. Every case must be judged on its own particular circumstances."

INFORMED CONSENT

A doctor must receive informed consent and will be found negligent where informed consent has not been obtained, and it is proven that had the plaintiff been informed he would not have gone through with the procedure.

Duty to Disclose

The duty to disclose arises before any medical treatment is undertaken. Informed consent is more than merely outlining the procedure to be undertaken, it requires an explanation of the procedure and its inherent risks. The extent of disclosure required however, is a question that has vexed the courts for a number of years. Traditionally, three approaches have been identified as to what a patient should be told and when. These approaches can be summarised as follows:

1. *Bolam* Test, (*Bolam v Friern Hospital Management Committee* [1957] 2 All E.R. 108). This test proposes that what the patient should be told is effectively a matter of medical judgment and discretion.
2. The patient must be told all material risks, in order to fully exercise their right to self-determination.
3. The *Dunne* test: essentially the *Bolam* test, except where disclosure of a particular risk is "so obviously necessary to an informed choice on the part of the patient that no reasonably prudent medical (person) would fail to make it." *Sidaway v Governors of the Bethlem Royal Hospital* [1985] A.C. 871 and *Dunne v National Maternity Hospital* [1989] I.R. 91.

The position in Ireland was considered in *Walsh v Family Planning Services* [1992] 1 I.R. 486. The case involved an elective vasectomy operation which left the patient with severe pain (orchialgia). While all judges were agreed that the risk should have been disclosed to the patient they were divided as to the principles governing disclosure. The majority however, did state that in "cases of elective surgery, where there is a risk, however exceptional or remote, of great consequence involving severe pain stretching for an appreciable time into the future and involving future operative procedures, such possible consequences should be explained in the clearest language to the prospective patient."

The position has been clarified to some extent, particularly in the case of elective surgery, by the more recent decisions in *Geoghegan v Harris* [2000] 3 I.R. 526 and *Fitzpatrick v White* [2007] I.E.S.C. 51 with Kearns J. delivering the High Court judgement in *Geoghegan* and the lead judgement in *Fitzpatrick*. In *Geoghegan* the patient had undergone a dental implant procedure which had left him with severe neurapathic pain. The dentist who carried out the procedure stated that he felt that only risks above 1 per cent ought to be disclosed, it had not occurred to him that the instant in question involved a sufficiently serious risk. Kearns J. held that the duty was to give a warning of any *material risk* which was a "known complication" of an operative procedure properly carried out. "Materiality" included consideration of both the severity of the consequences and the statistical frequency of the risk. As stated by Kearns J. "... every case must be considered in the light of its own particular facts, evidence and circumstances to see if the reasonable patient in the plaintiff's position would have required a warning of the particular risk." While this did not mean that material risks had to be disclosed in all cases, Kearns J. stated that the cases where full disclosure was not necessary would be "few in number" as disclosure in all cases might in the end be "counter productive if it needlessly deters patients from undergoing operations which are in their best interest to have."

This largely patient-centred approach was confirmed in *Fitzpatrick* which again involved an elective procedure, this time to correct a squint in the patient's eye. In the view of Kearns J., the "patient-centred" approach which advocates that patients ought to be informed of risks was to be preferred. In terms of the nature of any disclosure Kearns J. outlined the following principles:

1. Risks involving severe pain stretching for an appreciable time into the future and involving future operative procedures should be disclosed,
2. In cases not involving risks of severe ongoing pain, significant or material risks which would affect the judgment of a reasonable patient, should in the ordinary course of events, be disclosed,
3. Materiality involved a consideration of both (a) the statistical frequency of the risk and (b) the severity of the consequences, or otherwise put, whether a reasonable patient would attach significance to it.

The *Fitzpatrick* case also concerned the timing of any warning given. In that case a warning was given to the patient but only 30 minutes before the procedure was to be carried out. The plaintiff argued that this rendered the warning ineffective. The court disagreed however,

Kearns J. stating that while a warning given shortly before an operation was undesirable, the real consideration was whether it prevented the patient from being able to understand the nature of the warning given.

Causation and Informed Consent

Once it has been established that sufficient disclosure has not taken place the plaintiff must also establish that had they been fully informed they would not have gone ahead with the procedure (causation). Two broad approaches in reaching a decision are possible—the objective test which looks simply at what a reasonable person would have done in the circumstances (favoured in America and Canada), or the subjective test which looks at the character of the patient (favoured in some English decisions and in Australia). In *Geoghegan* Kearns J. opted for an approach which involved elements of both approaches requiring both an objective examination of whether a reasonable person in the plaintiff's position (given health, age, nature of the surgery (elective or compulsory) and so on) would have undergone the treatment and then a subjective inquiry of what the patient would have done, taking into account credible evidence (such as conversations with the doctor, or third parties and the conduct of the plaintiff him/herself). In the Geoghegan case, Kearns J. concluded that the patient would still have undergone the treatment, given the remote risk and the willingness of the patient to undergo the operation. In *Fitzpatrick* the issue of causation did not arise. While Kearns J. referred to an objective test, he did not disturb his earlier decision in *Geoghegan*.

BATTERY OR NEGLIGENCE?

Neglecting to obtain the consent of a patient before treatment constitutes a battery (unlawful touching without consent). The consent will be valid provided that the patient has been informed in broad terms about the nature of the treatment. If the patient has not been informed in this manner then any treatment of them is a trespass in the form of a battery. On the other hand, failing to receive informed consent constitutes not a battery but a case in medical negligence, as outlined above.

11. TRESPASS

INTRODUCTION

Most of the torts dealt with in this book are unintentional torts where damage is unintentional or accidental, or arises as a secondary result. These unintentional torts have historically been termed actions "on the case". Trespass however is one of the exceptions. It is an "intentional" tort, concerned with deliberate interference with the rights of another. It is one of the oldest established torts, based on a writ of trespass which originated in medieval times. The tort of trespass can arise when a person trespasses against another person, trespasses onto land or causes trespass to chattels (goods).

CHARACTERISTICS OF THE TORT OF TRESPASS

An action is trespass exists where the "trespass" arises from a direct impact brought about by a voluntary, intentional act. Trespass is also *actionable per se* in that it does not require proof of damage. The existence of damage however, will be taken into consideration when assessing compensation. It is noteworthy also that liability will arise for all damage flowing from the trespass and not simply for that damage which is foreseeable.

Direct Impact

The trespass or injury must be brought about by a "direct impact" i.e. the harm must flow directly from the act and not be merely consequential. It is however, notoriously difficult to state what a "direct" as opposed to "indirect" impact is. Take for example the case of injury from impact with a bag. If it arises because someone swings the bag and hits you, then this is clearly a direct impact. On the other hand if you simply trip over the bag causing injury this would support an action in negligence only. Other examples of direct impact would include chasing cattle onto land (trespass to land), being struck by a car (battery), being confined in a room (false imprisonment).

Voluntary Act

Any act which brings about a trespass must be a voluntary one. Where an action is simply a reflex action it will not be seen to be a voluntary act. A legitimate act of self-defence can also render conduct involuntary, as in *Scott v Shepherd* (1773) All E.R. Rep 295. In this case a man threw a firecracker which had landed close by away from the crowd to avoid injury. The initial thrower was held responsible for injury ultimately caused.

Intention

For an action in trespass to succeed the plaintiff must prove that the defendant "intended" to bring the result about. This does not have the ordinary mean of intention, which often equates with a desire to bring about a particular outcome. Legally, desire is irrelevant, and a person will be held to have intended the natural and probable result of his actions. So for instance, a person who fires a gun into a busy corridor will be found to have legally intended any resulting injuries, regardless of a desire to injure anybody.

Unintentional Trespass

If intention cannot be established a defendant may still be liable if he or she can be shown to have been negligent in bringing about harm as a result of a "direct impact". This is referred to as negligent or unintentional trespass but it is unclear what the status of this tort is in Irish law. Geoghegan J. in *Devlin v Roche* [2002] 2 I.L.R.M. 192 for instance stated that "... it seems clear from the treatment of the subject in McMahon and Binchy, The Law of Torts, that the law relating to unintentional trespass is not settled in Ireland. Not only would there be the question as to whether negligence is an essential ingredient but also the question as to the onus of proof in relation to such negligence."

TRESPASS AGAINST THE PERSON

There are three torts contained within the general tort of trespass against the person. These are assault, battery and false imprisonment. It may be recalled from Chapter 1 that a right to a jury exists for trespass to the person actions (Courts Act 1988, s.1(3)(b)).

Assault

An assault is an act that places another person in reasonable apprehension of an immediate battery being committed upon him. No touching needs to take place for an assault to occur. Gesticulating wildly, threatening movements and the brandishing of a gun are all capable of constituting an assault. All that is required is that the victim is in reasonable fear of a battery become committed upon him or her in the very near future. Shaking a fist at someone in a passing train while on the platform for instance, will not constitute an assault as it lacks immediacy.

In general, words will not amount to an assault unless they are accompanied by actions which could be perceived as a possible assault. As stated by Fawsitt J. in *Dullaghan v Hillen* [1957] Ir. Jur. Rep. 10 "mere words, no matter how harsh, lying, insulting and provocative they may be, can never amount in law to an assault." On the other hand, an otherwise threatening action can be made innocent by the use of words (*Tuberville v Savage* [1669] 86 E.R. 684).

Silence has also been held capable of constituting an assault as in *R v Ireland* [1998] A.C. 147. In this criminal law case a silent telephone caller was found guilty of assault as the victim apprehended physical contact as a result.

Assault in tort does not seem to encompass mental as well as physical assault but the law may be changing in this respect.

Battery

Battery is the direct application of physical contact upon the person of another without his or her consent, express or implied. There are a number of cases where contact can be less than entirely direct, spitting for example is also a battery. A plaintiff need not be aware that a battery is being committed upon them, leaning over for instance to kiss a sleeping fellow passenger is still a battery.

Implied consent to otherwise unlawful touching exists for a range of everyday events, such as minor bumping on a crowded bus, accidental touching in a busy lecture theatre or activities such as contact sports.

In cases of medical treatment a person is entitled to refuse medical treatment, even where this leads to death or serious injury and any forcing of treatment upon them will constitute a battery. An exception lies where the person in need of medical attention does not have capacity to consent, in which case consent may be given on their behalf, as in *F v West Berkshire Health Authority* [1990] 2 A.C. 1, where the court consented to the performance of a sterilization procedure on an adult patient deemed incapable of consent.

It has been held in a number of cases that consent does not extend to acts which are "hostile". Hostility has been described not as "ill-will or malevolence" (*Wilson v Pringle* [1987] Q.B. 237), but more an understanding by the defendant that she or he is doing something which the plaintiff may regard as an unlawful intrusion on the plaintiff's right to physical autonomy and privacy. So for example a person cannot "consent" to a fist fight in public, as this is seen to be hostile act. On the other hand, in the case of *Wilson* (above) consent was held to exist in the case of a young boy injured in "horseplay" with another boy. Consent existed in this case as the horseplay was held to lack hostility.

False Imprisonment

In *Dullaghan v Hillen* [1957] Ir. Jur. Rep. 10 false imprisonment was described by Fawsitt J. as "the unlawful and total restraint of the personal liberty of another whether by constraining him or compelling him to go to a particular place or by confining him … against his will". The victim need not be aware of his or her detention. Restraint requires that the victim cannot reasonably escape confinement, there is no expectation that the victim needs to injure himself, or suffer unreasonable humiliation in order to escape.

The imprisonment may be physical or psychological. Psychological restraint would exist where a person fears that force will be used to confine him or her if he or she does not comply. However, if a person can escape confinement through reasonable means there is no false imprisonment. In *Phillips v GN Ry Co Ltd* (1903) 4 N.I.J.R. 154 the plaintiff was temporarily delayed by the stationmaster from leaving the train-station in a taxi as he suspected some difficulty with her ticket. Following an exchange of words which lasted a few minutes she left by taxi. No false imprisonment was found as the court held that while the plaintiff had experienced "some delay" she had not "lost her liberty".

The detention must be such as to limit the victim's freedom of motion in all directions; the extent of the limitation may vary, from an area as small as a lavatory to a large building. But is would seem unlikely to extend to a county, or a country, see *Louis v Commonwealth* (1986) 87 F.L.R. 277.

Failure to release someone may constitute false imprisonment, where the defendant has undertaken a commitment to release. However, if a person may leave on satisfying certain reasonable conditions and they refuse to do so then no false imprisonment issues arise (see *Burns v Johnston* [1919] 2 I.R. 444 where an employee who could have left work by asking for a key to unlock a gate, was held not be falsely imprisoned).

TRESPASS TO LAND

Trespass onto land arises where someone intentionally or negligently enters, remains on or causes anything to be placed onto land in the possession of another, without lawful justification.

The slightest entry without lawful justification will amount to a trespass, and in some cases even physical contact with the perimeter of the land will suffice, as in *Whelan v Madigan* [1978] I.L.R.M. 136, where the High Court found that striking a door with the intention of breaking it amounted to a trespass.

A person may also enter lawfully but become a trespasser if they remain on land after their right to remain has ceased (see below under *trespass ab initio* for further implications of this principle).

Finally, a person may be liable for trespass where they place any object on the land of another, or cause any object or substance to cross the boundary of another's land, or even to reach the boundary. They must actively cause it to happen, so for instance chasing sheep onto another's land or throwing rocks onto it will constitute trespass. Merely leaving a gate open so that sheep stray onto land however, will lack the necessary directness to constitute trespass.

What is Land?

Land includes that attached to the land and all the soil beneath the land, all its contents and all of the space above it. However, this general principle is limited to that which is required to allow the possessor of land enjoyment of it.

Dwellings in particular are afforded special protection by virtue of Art.40.5 of the Constitution, which states that the dwelling of every citizen is inviolable save where entry is permitted by law. In *The People (Attorney General) v O'Brien* [1965] I.R. 169 it was held that entry onto a premises without a warrant could only be allowed where "… extraordinary excusing circumstances" existed, examples given included imminent destruction of evidence or the need to rescue someone in danger.

Lawful Justification

Trespass onto land occurs where the interference arises without lawful justification. Lawful justification can be obtained from statute or by virtue of the common law. For instance under the common law a search warrant may be issued by a District Justice or Peace Commissioner where reasonable grounds exist. There is also a right to enter unto land in the interests of "social necessity" but this is interpreted quite strictly.

An array of legislation also provides for the right of entry onto private property including legislation which allows a right to enter to prevent or investigate criminal behaviour (e.g. to investigate violations of health and safety legislation (Safety, Health and Welfare at Work Act 2005) and to carry out essential services (e.g. Arterial Drainage (Amendment) Act 1995).

Where an entrant exceeds their lawful authority to enter, then they will become a trespasser. In *DPP v McMahon* [1987] I.L.R.M. 87, Gardaí who entered a premises without a search warrant were found to be in abuse of their right to enter to investigate a violation under the Gaming and Lotteries Act 1956. In law therefore they were trespassers.

Trespass ab initio

In some cases remaining on land after your right to be there has elapsed will make you a trespasser not merely from the moment that you no longer have a right to be there, but from when you first entered. This is known as the concept of *trespass ab initio* or trespass from the beginning. It will only arise if your right to be on the land comes from a lawful authority and you have no other valid reason for being on the land (*Elias v Pasmore* [1934] 2 K.B. 164). It also requires the trespasser to do a positive act (misfeasance), which renders the presence on land unlawful. So for instance if a member of the Gardaí comes onto property with a warrant to investigate gaming offences, they become trespassers *ab initio* if they subsequently seize documents in relation to drugs offences.

Historically, if the right to be on land comes from the express or implied consent of the possessor, then the entrant does not become a trespasser from the beginning, but only a trespasser from the moment they exceed your authority. It is uncertain that this is such a clear rule today as there is some evidence that the public/private distinction may be waning. See for instance *Webb v Ireland* [1988] I.R. 353, where two people who came onto property with the implied right of the owners to visit a church and tomb used the opportunity to dig for treasure. Finlay C.J., stated in this case that they became "trespassers ab initio" when they started to dig, ignoring any distinction between public/private authority.

Possession of Another

The law does not protect the rights of those who own land but rather the rights of those in possession of it. Generally the person with possession is the owner, but this is not always the case. In cases where the owner exceeds his right to property the occupier may have a right to sue. In *Whelan v Madigan* [1978] I.L.R.M. 136 for instance, the landlord was held to have committed a trespass against the occupiers when he damaged the door and letter box.

In the case where a person establishes possession through exclusive occupation or use of the property they are referred to as being in de facto possession of the land. While renting a property clearly gives the necessary degree of possession, renting a hotel room does not as the possession lacks the necessary degree of exclusive occupation or use. De facto possessors of land can sue others in trespass provided there is no authority from a lawful owner for the act at issue. In the case of *Petrie v Owners of SS Rostrevor* [1898] 2 I.R. 556, Petrie had placed oysters on the foreshore. The defendant's vessel had run aground and damaged the oyster beds. The question arose as to whether Petrie had an action against them in trespass. The court held that "by placing the oysters on the foreshore (he had) become possessed of it *de facto* as against all the world except its true owner." As it happened, there was a lawful owner, from whom the vessel owners had authority to use the foreshore, in which case Petrie could not recover.

TRESASS TO CHATTELS

Trespass to chattels is defined as the "deliberate use or otherwise interference with a chattel in the possession of another without lawful authority." Again, trespass must involve direct impact, and be the result of a voluntary, intentional or negligent act on the part of the defendant.

Touching another's personal property may suffice, moving it, damaging it in some way or taking it out of the owner's possession, would all constitute trespass.

Possession of Another

As with trespass to land the law is not concerned with protecting those in ownership but rather those in possession. An action therefore may also lie against the owner, where s/he exceeds his lawful authority over a good. In the case of *Keenan Bros Ltd v CIE* (1963) 97 I.L.T.R. 54 the owners of goods which were delayed in train wagons were not allowed to enter the wagons to remove the goods without the permission of CIE and in the absence of any contractual right to do so. If they had so entered, they themselves would be liable for trespass.

Position of Chattels Found

The position of items found is not entirely clear as the issue has not been completely addressed in Irish law. The leading Irish case is that of *Webb v Ireland* [1988] I.R. 353. This case involved two persons who came onto property with the implied right of the owners to visit a church and tomb. They however, used the opportunity to dig, exceeding their authority to enter and came upon the Derrynaflan Hoard (valuable chalices). A dispute then ensued as to who the true owners of the find were.

Finlay C.J. ultimately resolved the issue as follows:

- In general the true owner of a find has a superior right over all others;
- In the absence of a true owner, the owner of land on which property is found will have a superior right over all others where the item is attached to the land, under the land, or partially submerged in the land;
- If the item is found on the land, and the land owner has not asserted a claim over it, then the finder may have a superior right if he or she was lawfully on the land at the time he or she found it.
- A necessary ingredient of sovereignty of a modern State is that the State should be the owner of objects which constitute antiquities of importance and who have no other true owner. The court rejected that the right of the royal prerogative of treasure trove, which derived from the crown, had survived the establishment of the Irish Free State.

However, in this case as the plaintiffs had been promised by the National Museum that they would be "honourably treated" the court ruled that they had a legitimate expectation and were thus awarded £25,000 each as an equitable solution.

DEFENCES TO TRESPASS

The principal defences to an action in trespass are as follows:

- Consent,
- Defence of Person or Property,
- Necessity,
- Discipline,
- Lawful Authority.

Consent

The effect of consent is to render contact lawful (it is not strictly speaking a defence) and is based on the maxim of *volenti non fit injuria* (no wrong is done to one who consents). Consent however, is no defence unless it is given to the precise conduct in question or at least to acts of a substantially similar nature. Consent given may be express or implied (implied either by a persons actions, by custom or by statute).

In order for consent to be valid the person who gives consent must have capacity to do so. It is generally accepted that an adult has the capacity to give valid consent. It is for the party arguing that an adult does not have capacity to prove such incapacity (*F v West Berkshire Health Authority* [1990] 2 A.C. 1 (HL)). Minors have capacity to consent if it can be shown that they possess the intellectual and emotional capacity to comprehend the nature and consequences of what is proposed. Where the limit lies in this respect is difficult to determine. In the English case of *Gillick v West Norfold and Wisbech Area Health Authority* [1986] A.C. 112, the right of a minor to obtain contraceptives without parental consent was upheld. It is a matter for future determination if Irish courts would find likewise. If minors are not deemed to have the capacity to consent, then parental consent is required.

In some cases the consent of a third party may be accepted, where it is deemed necessary to preserve life and health. This arose in the case of *Holmes v Heatley* [1937] Ir. Jur. Rep. 74, where a boy who underwent an operation involving the use of a local anesthetic had to be administered a general anesthetic in the course of the operation. He subsequently died. In this case however, the court found that the surgeon was bound to act as he did given the emergency he faced.

In the criminal law (which may be of some guidance when considered the civil defence of consent) s.23 of the Non-Fatal Offences against the Person Act 1997 provides that where a minor over the age of 16 gives "effective" consent to a surgical operation, then the consent of the parents is not necessary. There is no mention of those under 16 but this does not necessarily mean that they can never give consent.

In medical cases it was stated by O'Flaherty J. in *Walsh v Family Planning Services Ltd* [1992] 1 I.R. 496 that "A claim of assault should be confined to cases where there is no consent to the particular procedure and where it is feasible to look for a consent." Where no express consent is given a practitioner must show that an urgent need existed, such as in the case of *Holmes* above.

Consent may be invalidated where it was obtained through a fraud or through duress. The general principle is that fraud as to the nature and quality of the act will vitiate consent, whereas fraud as to some other collateral matter e.g. physical attributes, the purpose of contact and so on will not. In the criminal case of *Papadimitropoulous v R* (1957) 98 C.L.R. 249, a woman who engaged in sexual intercourse in the mistaken belief that she was married to the man in question, was none-the-less found to have consented to the act of intercourse, the moral nature of it being a "collateral" matter. In some cases fraud as to an element that would appear "collateral" will be held to vitiate consent, when note is taken of plaintiff's age and experience and the position of the defendant. In the criminal case of *R v Williams* [1923] 1 K.B. 340, for instance a choir master who tricked a girl to have intercourse with him by making her believe that it would improve her voice was found guilty.

While these criminal cases serve as a good guide, the position in the civil law is still in a state of development. There have been some cases which indicate that the courts are taking a more plaintiff friendly approach. In the case of *Norberg v Wynrib* (1992) 92 D.L.R. for instance, a woman who was a drug addict agreed to sexual intercourse with a doctor in exchange for supplying her with drugs. She was allowed to recover in tort, on the ground that consent was vitiated by undue influence.

Controversial in recent years has been the case of knowingly infecting or risking the infection of a partner with a sexually transmitted disease. One of the first major cases in this area was that of *Hegarty v Shine* (1878) 4 L.R. (Ir.) 288, where a man who infected his partner was not found guilty of battery. There is some evidence that the unmarried nature of their relationship was also a factor. However, recently in Canada and more historically in America, liability has been attached to those who knowingly infect another party with a sexual transmitted disease.

Defence of Persons or Property

Reasonable force may be used for the protection or persons or property. This is also stated in s.8(a) of the Occupiers Liability Act 1995. What is reasonable depends on the risk which is being protected against, and the surrounding circumstances. Where violence has been used to effect the trespass reasonable force may be used to counter it, on the other hand where no force or violence has been used, a request must be made before the other party can resort to physical violence. In the case of *MacKnight v Xtravision*, Circuit Court, July 5, 1991, it was held that the force used was unreasonable in the circumstances. In this case a dispute arose between the plaintiff and another driver over a parking space in a shopping center. The plaintiff was asked by the security officer to leave, but he refused to do so, allegedly punched the security guard and demanded to see the manager. The plaintiff alleged that he was assaulted, carried, pulled and dragged by the security officers and brought to a small room where he was detained until the guards arrived. He had himself wished that the guards be called. Spain J. held that reasonableness was the criterion and that the reaction of the security staff had been excessive.

Necessity

Necessity differs from self defence in that it involves trespass against a person or their property who is not in any way responsible for creating the threat or the need themselves. It requires "an urgent situation of imminent peril", and all actions must be reasonable and proportionate. Generally it involves damage to property. It provides a defence for say, a "public champion", such as fire-fighters or other public workers, who damage property in order to prevent greater harm, and in some cases the protection of private interests where this is deemed to prevent a greater harm. It has also been applied in cases of medical interventions such as *Holmes v Heatley* [1937] Ir. Jur. Rep. 74 and *F v Berkshire Health Authority* [1990] 2 A.C. 1 above.

Discipline

Reasonable discipline may be a defence but only in the event of children or possibly in other appropriate cases to maintain order. With respect to children the defence extends to parents or those in loco parentis (although it is the belief of the Law Reform Commission and one which they had initially wished to incorporate into the Non-Fatal Offences Against the Persons Act 1997 that this right be abolished). Corporal punishment in schools has been abolished (s.24 of the above Act), but detaining children after school is still permissible. In all cases the disciplinary measure employed needs to be proportionate to the objective or need.

Lawful Authority

The Gardaí have wide powers of arrest and arrest and detention, powers to enter property and the power to seize property. If Gardaí exceed their authority in exercising any of these powers however, it will constitute a trespass. Private citizens also have restricted powers to arrest and detain individuals, again if this power is exceeded it will constitute a trespass. Other examples of lawful authority are discussed above in relation to trespass to land.

12. NUISANCE

INTRODUCTION

The scope of the tort of nuisance is notoriously difficult to define. It covers all those wrongs arising from unreasonable interference with another's rights, generally connected to land. It covers a wide range of harm from pollution cases and excessive noise to blocking a highway and keeping a brothel.

DEFINITION

In *Connolly v South of Ireland Asphalt Co* [1977] I.R. 99, O'Higgins C.J. described nuisance as follows:

> "It has been said that actionable nuisance is incapable of exact definition. The term nuisance contemplates an act or omission, which amounts to an unreasonable interference with, disturbance of, or annoyance to another person in the exercise of his rights. If the rights so interfered with belong to the person as a member of the public, the act or omission is a public nuisance. If these rights relate to the ownership of land, or of some easement, profit or other right enjoyed in connection with land, then the acts or omissions amount to a private nuisance."

A central requirement therefore is that there is interference and that this interference is unreasonable. Nuisance can be of two types, private nuisance or public nuisance. Private nuisance covers those cases involving the unreasonable interference with a person's right to the use and enjoyment of their land. Public nuisance goes beyond occupancy of land, and covers situations where a person has been subject to an obstruction, inconvenience or damage in the exercise of rights which are common to all (such as when a person is on the public highway). The essential difference between the two types of nuisance is that the individual in a private nuisance case has an interest in the land, while in the case of public nuisance no such interest lies. In all cases the longer an interference continues the more likely it will be deemed to constitute a nuisance.

BASIS FOR LIABILITY

Generally speaking in nuisance cases no evidence of negligence on the part of the defendant is required, in this sense it is a strict liability tort. It therefore differs from and is more advantageous than an action in negligence, where breach of duty of care is a requisite element. There is an exception however, when the injury comes about because of a failure to act. In these cases the exercise of reasonable care may be a defence (see below under private nuisance and physical injury to land). This has led some commentators to suggest that the line between nuisance and negligence is becoming increasingly blurred.

The damage must also be foreseeable. As stated by Walsh J., in *Wall v Morrissey* [1969] I.R. 10: "While negligence is not a essential ingredient of nuisance in an action on public nuisance, foreseeability is an essential ingredient."

REMEDIES

Nuisance, unlike negligence, can result in an action for not only damages but also an injunction. This is because in many nuisance cases, such as noise or overhanging branches, damages would not be an appropriate remedy.

An injunction is an order of the court directing a person to refrain from doing or continuing an act or ordering them to carry out a remedial action. It is, however, an equitable remedy and as such it is at the discretion of the court as to whether an injunction is granted.

In certain cases it will also be permissible for the claimant to abate the nuisance. It is restricted to nuisances such as overhanging branches or in cases of emergency. In all cases the abatement must be reasonable.

PUBLIC NUISANCE

As stated above public nuisance covers situations where a person has been subjected to an unreasonable interference where they do not have an interest in the land. When the public or a section of it is injured by an act of public nuisance, only the Attorney General can litigate in civil proceedings. The reasons for this are twofold. First, as it is an interference that affects the public as a whole, it could lead to a very large number of litigants pursuing actions, which in turn would lead to a clogging up of the courts system. Secondly, it could lead to a situation where a person would risk being subjected to endless litigation arising from the same act. This reasoning is at odds with general negligence principles however, where such concerns for the position of the defendant do not feature.

Where a person can show "special damage", over and above that suffered by other members of the public, then the way is open to take a personal action.

Incidences of nuisance include pollution (but there is a particular difficulty in pursing an individual action on this basis), rock concerts, obstructions on the highway (such as pickets, marches) noise and so on. Digging a trench in a highway is also capable of constituting a public nuisance (*Wall v Morrissey* [1969] I.R. 10) as is leaving a ladder unattended where a member of the public could trip over it (*Cunningham v McGrath Brothers* [1964] I.R. 209).

Special Damage

It is difficult to lay down a clear rule as to what constitutes special damage. Some argue that it must be different not only in degree, but also in kind, to that suffered by the general public. This, it appears, is the position in Canada. In Ireland however (and in England) the view is that where a plaintiff can show injury to pecuniary interests, property, person, or ability to earn a living, which is appreciably more serious than that suffered by the general public, they are allowed to pursue an action independently. It appears that the fact that the damage could be suffered by a number of people will not bar an action.

In *Smith v Wilson* [1903] 2 I.R. 45 (KBD) the plaintiff, who was prevented from using a public road to walk to a market in Ballymena, succeeded in showing special damage. The defendant blocked the road by removing a bridge and erecting a fence. The elderly farmer had to take a much longer route to the market, sometimes having to pay a car to do so. In finding that he was entitled to damages, Gibson J. held that:

"I think there is some evidence on which a jury might find that the plaintiff had sustained peculiar, direct and substantial damage in farm business, and expenses. ... Everyone who individually sustains particular injury can apply for damages or an injunction."

Private Nuisance

Private nuisance is the unreasonable interference with rights related to the ownership or occupation of land. The law will protect against any unreasonable interference so long as the requirements of the plaintiff also are reasonable. As stated in *Hanrahan v Merck, Sharp & Dohme (Ireland) Ltd* [1988] I.L.R.M. 629,

> "... what an occupier of land is entitled to as against his neighbour, is the comfortable and healthy enjoyment of the land to the degree that would be expected by an ordinary person whose requirements are objectively reasonable in all the particular circumstances."

In terms of what the court deems to be reasonable Henchy J. went on to say that:

> "To my mind the reasonable man connotes a person whose notions and standards of behaviour and responsibility correspond with those generally pertaining among ordinary people in our society at the present time, who seldom allows his emotions to overbear his reason, whose habits are moderate and whose disposition is equable."

Nuisance and Trespass

Private nuisance is distinguishable from trespass in that the latter involves a direct impact, while in the former the damage is merely consequential. For instance if one points a water spout at another's land and floods it, that will be a trespass in that the impact is direct. However, if a water pipe is constructed in such a way that the water eventually (and as a consequence of the pipe) flows onto a neighbour's land then it is a nuisance. Generally trespass involves intrusions by tangible objects, be they persons or things, and constitute physical acts done unto the plaintiff's land. Although the distinction is not always a clear one (for example the intrusion of branches and roots have always been seen as nuisance and not trespass) it is important as the legal requirements differ. For trespass no damage is required (it is *actionable per se*) whereas for nuisance proof of damage is required.

Unreasonable Interference

Unreasonable interference can be physical interference to land or buildings (for example by vibrations, intrusions, flooding, fire and so on) or an unreasonable interference with a right to a person's enjoyment of their own property (through for example offensive smells, noise, smoke, dust, causing reasonable fear for ones' safety or health, or offending morals).

Interestingly some rights are not protected, such as the right to a view, nor is there an absolute right to light. Interfering however, with property rights such as easements or *profits à prendre* (the right to take something off another's land) will also amount to a nuisance.

Physical Injury to Land

A person is liable for a nuisance constituted by the state of their property either by causing the physical injury through a positive act (such as allowing noxious gases to leave your premises and injure a nearby property) or by neglect of some duty which allows the injury to arise (such as neglecting to cut back trees which encroach onto a neighbour's property). The courts have increasingly referred to the reasonableness of the defendant's actions when contemplating the former (causing the nuisance by a positive act). For instance in the case of *Hanrahan v Merck, Sharp & Dohme (Ireland) Ltd* [1988] I.L.R.M. 629, Henchy J. in the Supreme Court stated that to establish liability the plaintiffs were required to show,

> "… that they have been interfered with, over a substantial period of time, in the use and enjoyment of their farm, as a result of the way the defendants conducted their operations in the factory. The plaintiffs do not have to prove want of reasonable care on the part of the defendants."

In the *Hanrahan* case, the plaintiffs complained that their health and that of their livestock had been damaged by emissions from a nearby factory.

However where the damage has arisen due to a failure to act, the courts give regard to whether the defendants have taken reasonable care. For instance in the case of *Daly & Daly v McMullan*, unreported, Circuit Court, Buckley J., April 11, 1997 the court refused to impose liability on the defendants without first hearing evidence as to whether they had taken "reasonable care". The plaintiffs in this case occupied a house that bordered on the defendant's property. The action arose out of damage caused by soil from the defendant's property falling down an embankment onto the property of the plaintiffs. A similar outcome was recorded in the case of *Lynch v Hetherton* [1990] I.L.R.M. 857. In this case an ash tree fell on the plaintiff's car while he was driving along a country road. The farmer in question regularly inspected the trees and the fact that the tree was completely rotten from the inside was not reasonably visible. In finding no liability Hanlon J., stated that: "I consider that the defendant exercised the degree of care that would have been exercised by a reasonable and prudent landowner."

Such findings weaken the strict liability nature of nuisance cases but appear to be restricted to where the defendant has not caused injury from a positive act.

A Substantial Interference with the Enjoyment of Land

A person can also be liable for private nuisance where they unreasonably interfere with another's right to the quiet enjoyment of their land. This interference was described in *Patterson v Murphy* [1978] I.L.R.M. 85, as "personal inconvenience and interference with one's enjoyment, one's quiet, one's personal freedom, anything that discomposes or injuriously affects the senses or the nerves."

The central requirement is that the conduct of the defendant is "unreasonable". In determining this issue the courts have traditionally sought to strike a balance between the utility of the defendant's conduct and the gravity of the harm likely to result from the conduct at issue. Other important factors are the location in which the nuisance arises and the behaviour of the plaintiff. Provided that the conduct is not completely without merit the courts will not generally prohibit it in its entirety. Rather they will see to strike a compromise between the competing interests of both the plaintiff and the defendant.

Utility of the Conduct

The greater the utility of the defendant's conduct the less likely the courts are to prohibit it. Many activities capable of constituting a nuisance, such as running a bar, playing music or providing a 24-hour service, have some merit. However, the rights of those living in proximity to such activities must also be respected. In the case of

Clifford v Drug Treatment Centre Board, High Court, McCracken J., November 7, 1997, the court succeeded in balancing competing interests. The plaintiffs in this case objected to the operation and expansion of a treatment centre for drug addicts as they argued that it interfered with the running of their business. In declining to grant an injunction reducing the number of drug addicts, McCracken J. stated that to do so would go "clearly against the public interest, besides depriving possibly hundreds of individuals of badly needed treatment." As a compromise however he did award an injunction to prevent further expansion of the centre.

Location

In deciding whether the behaviour is "unreasonable" the courts will also look to the nature of the area in which the nuisance takes place. Running a busy bar or nightclub in the center of a city for instance will be tolerated whereas the same activity in a residential area might well constitute an actionable nuisance. In the case of *Molumby v Kearns*, High Court, O'Sullivan J., January 19, 1999, the location in which the nuisance arose was central in the decision of the court. The plaintiffs sought an injunction restraining the activities of a nearby industrial estate that operated on a 24-hour basis. As the industrial estate was located near a residential area the court ordered that the industrial estate operate only within normal working hours from Monday to Friday and to Saturday mornings as a way of reconciling both interests. Similarly in the case of *O'Kane v Campbell* [1985] I.R. 115, a 24-hour shop on the corner of a busy street and a residential area was required to restrict business hours rather than to close completely, to accommodate the needs of elderly residents in the area.

Sensitivity of the Defendant

Not only must the activity of the defendant be reasonable but the demands of the plaintiff must also be that of a reasonable person before they can seek a remedy in nuisance. Unreasonable sensitivities or unusual demands will rarely be entertained. For this reason no liability was imposed in the case of *Robinson v Kilvert* (1889) 41 Ch. D. 88. The defendant, Kilvert, carried out a business of manu-facturing paper boxes for which he needed his flat to be heated to a high temperature. This in turn damaged heat sensitive paper held in the plaintiff's flat. No liability was imposed for this potential nuisance, as the plaintiff was not entitled to be compensated for a loss arising from what the court described as an "exceptionally delicate trade".

Who may Sue for Private Nuisance

Traditionally the view was that only those with a proprietary interest in land could sue in an action for private nuisance. This right has now been extended to give occupiers and in some cases family members (as in *Hanrahan*) who have been affected by the nuisance, the right to bring an action. The plaintiff however, must be either in "ownership or occupation" of the land in question. It is unlikely therefore that someone who is merely on the land at the time of the nuisance could bring an action. In *Hunter v Canary Wharf Ltd* [1997] 2 W.L.R. 685 for instance, it was restated that only a person with an interest in the land or premises may sue for private nuisance. The House of Lords felt that such a limitation was necessary to protect the character of this particular tort.

Who may be Sued?

The creator of the nuisance or anyone who authorises the nuisance by failing to take reasonable steps to abate the nuisance can be sued. In this way the landlord who leases or rents a premises with a nuisance or who fails to repair a premises leading to a nuisance, may be liable. In *Goldfarb v Williams & Co* [1945] I.R. 433 for instance, the premises had been let to an employees' social and athletic club, which operated dances and other social activities. As the building was by its construction unsuitable for such a purpose, the landlord was found liable as by renting it they were held to have authorised the nuisance. An occupier (anyone in control of the premises) may also be sued where they create or again, where they authorise the nuisance. An occupier may be said to have authorised the nuisance where he or she has failed to remove it within a reasonable time of becoming aware of it.

Defences

Most of the general defences apply (such as consent and contributory negligence). In addition, there are two special defences that apply to the area of nuisance. These are:

- Statutory authority;
- Prescription.

Statutory Authority

The defence of statutory authority arises where the defendant can show that the nuisance is an inevitable consequence of the performance of an activity authorised by statute. If however, the nuisance is not inevitable, but results from negligence or from a failure to use a less intrusive method, the defence will fail. Similarly in planning cases, inevitable interruptions will not constitute nuisance. In *Superquinn Ltd v Bray Urban District Council*, unreported, High Court, Laffoy J., February 18, 1998, the substantive proceedings arose from catastrophic flooding in Bray. The council was sued in nuisance as they had carried out drainage works (pursuant to the Public Health (Ireland) Act 1878), which the plaintiffs argued had interfered with the flow of the river and with its defences. In finding the council not liable Laffoy J. held that "the Council is immune from an action based on nuisance and is free from liability unless it was negligent in the exercise of its statutory duty and power." There was no evidence of any negligent behaviour and the action failed.

Prescription

Prescription refers to the acquisition (or extinction) of rights brought about by continuous use without objection and can be a defence in private nuisance actions only. The defendant must prove that he has been acting openly and with the knowledge of the plaintiff. In certain cases a continuation of an activity after 20 years will legalise an activity which might otherwise constitute a nuisance. Some activities however, are incapable of being legalised by prescription such as the intrusion of branches or roots onto another's property. Also, an activity which by its nature varies, such as levels or noise or dust and is therefore not uniformly continuous, will be unlikely to attract the defence of prescription.

Ineffectual Defences

It will not be a defence to claim that the plaintiff "came to the nuisance". This might be claimed for instance where a person knowingly moves next door to a noisy neighbour, or buys a house with overhanging branches from a neighbour's garden. A person comes to an area with all of their rights attached, including the right to sue in nuisance (*Bliss v Hall* (1838) 4 Bing NC 183, 132 E.R. 758).

13. *RYLANDS V FLETCHER*

INTRODUCTION

The principle enunciated in the case of *Rylands v Fletcher* (1868) L.R. 3 H.L. 330 deals with the imposition of liability for what amounts to a dangerous use of property. As it covers liability or interference in relation to land there is a degree of overlap with nuisance and for many years the courts treated it as a specialised form of nuisance, but with a different basis of liability and without the requirement of continuity. Today, however, the tort of nuisance and what is referred to simply as the rule in *Rylands v Fletcher (R v F)*, are seen are separate torts.

THE RULE IN *RYLANDS V FLETCHER*

The rule in *R v F* imposes liability where the defendant brings onto his or her land a non-natural thing and causes injury by allowing that thing to escape. As the tort is named after the case in which it was developed, it is important that we look to the facts of the case for clarification. The defendants were mill owners and engaged independent contractors to build a reservoir. Unbeknownst to them the independent contractors built the reservoir over a disused mine shaft, which collapsed causing water to escape and to flood the plaintiff's coal mine. The plaintiffs sued in nuisance, negligence and trespass for the injury they had suffered, ultimately failing under all three headings. With respect to nuisance, the court found that the incident lacked continuity. It was not trespass as the flow of water onto the land was not a direct impact/consequence. Finally, with respect to negligence, the court found that the defendants could not be found liable for the negligent act of the independent contractor (this however is not always the case today). Despite the fact that the case did not fit into any of the traditional areas of tort liability, and possibly swayed by the considerable loss suffered by the plaintiff, (or as suggested by some commentators, to protect miners against the emerging millers), liability was imposed on the defendant.

In imposing liability, Lord Blackburn stated:

"We think that the true rule of law is, that the person who for his own purposes brings on his lands and collects and keeps there anything likely to do mischief if it escapes, must keep it in at his peril, and, if he does not do so, is prima facie answerable for all the damage which is the natural consequences of its escape."

The case was not received enthusiastically in all jurisdictions, partly due to the difficulties of classifying when an activity amounted to an unnatural use and the resulting strict liability which would then be imposed.

There are a number of elements to the rule in *R v F*. They are as follows:

- Non-natural use of property
- Accumulation or collection of / Brought onto property
- Escape
- Damage
- Lack of Defence

NON-NATURAL USE

Before a plaintiff can rely on the rule in *R v F* he or she must show that the activities of the defendant are in some way unusual or out of the ordinary and constitute an increased danger for others. The definition of what is or is not a non-natural use is not a clear concept and has been the subject of much debate. The object in question does not have to be dangerous in or of itself, but it must be capable of causing injury if it escapes. While the escape does not have to be foreseeable, the potential that it will cause injury, must be. A wide range of activities can be covered. As stated by Lord Porter in *Read v J. Lyons & Co Ltd* [1947] A.C. 156: "Among dangerous objects have been held to be included gas, explosive substances, electricity, oil, fumes, rusty wire, poisonous vegetation, vibrations, a flag-pole, and even dwellers in caravans."

What constitutes a non-natural use is also affected by the passage of time or the place or other circumstances of the case. For instance, a vehicle with a petrol tank was thought to be a non-natural use in *Musgrove v Pandelis* [1919] 2 K.B. 43. It is unlikely of course that this would be the position today. Also in *R v F*, the accumulation of water in a reservoir was seen to be a non-natural use, but the accumulation of water on the other hand for irrigation purposes in an irrigation district would not.

As stated in *Read v J. Lyons & Co Ltd* [1947] A.C. 156, electricity, oil and gas can all amount to dangerous objects. Generally speaking when they are kept on property in quantities which correspond with that required for ordinary domestic purposes it will not be deemed to be a non-natural use. In *Miller v Addie & Sons (Collieries) Ltd* [1934] S.C. 150 for instance the escape of gas from pipes used to convey gas to domestic houses was not seen as a non-natural use of property. Once these substances are accumulated in large or commercial quantities however, they may amount to a non-natural use.

In some cases the public good will be considered. For instance a munitions factory in the Second World War was not seen to constitute an unnatural use of land (*Read v J. Lyons & Co Ltd* [1947] A.C. 156).

ACCUMULATION OR COLLECTION ONTO PROPERTY

The defendant must have accumulated the dangerous thing and brought the dangerous thing unto their property for liability to attach. No liability will arise for objects which occur naturally on the land, such as rainfall or groundwater, vegetation, soil or rocks. In the case of *Healy v Bray UDC* [1962–1963] Ir. Jur. Rep. 9, an escape of rocks from land which injured the plaintiff was held not to be covered by the rule in *R v F*. As stated by Kingsmill Moore,

> "The defendants did not bring the rocks or outcrop on to [their] land for their own purpose (or at all). They are there as the result of natural forces operating in geological time, as indeed is the land. They are, in short, the land itself and not things brought onto it."

The rule however, will apply to planted vegetation, reservoirs or even where naturally occurring rocks are scattered by explosives, *Miles v Forest Rock Granite Co (Leicestershire) Ltd* (1918) 34 T.L.R. 500. In this case the explosives were seen to be the accumulated item and as the rock thrown from the land was a foreseeable consequence then liability was imposed.

ESCAPE

According to Viscount Simon, in the case of *Read v J. Lyons* [1947] A.C. 156,

"... 'escape,' for the purpose of applying the proposition in *Rylands v Fletcher* means escape from a place where the defendant has occupation or 'control over land to a place, which is outside his occupation or control."

In the *Read* case, the plaintiff was an inspector of munitions, who was injured when a high explosive shell exploded when it was being manufactured at the defendant's factory. At the time the plaintiff was in the shell shop (a part of the factory). The plaintiff sought to rely on *R v F*, but this was rejected because there was not an escape from the place where the defendant had "occupation or control".

Generally speaking the escape will be from land but the principle also includes an escape from the highway. In *Rigby v Chief Constable of Northamptonshire* QBD [1985] 2 All E.R. 985, the police released gas into a shop to try and force out a dangerous psychopath who had broken in. The canister set the shop on fire and the plaintiffs, the owners of the shop, sought to recover. Taylor J. in this case accepted that escape applied equally to things brought onto the highway and allowed to escape (as in *Rigby*).

DAMAGE

Damage appears to be an essential element of the tort, the only situation where damage is not necessary is where a preventative injunction is being sought, i.e. a *quia timet* injunction.

Those entitled to sue under the rule in *R v F* include the occupier of the land and as in nuisance those with an interest in the land. Unlike the position in England, the Irish authorities seem to suggest that a non-occupier could also recover for personal injuries (as in *Healy v Bray UDC* above).

The plaintiff can recover for any physical damage and associated economic loss. In relation to personal injury the English courts have ruled out the possibility of recovery for this type of injury, *Transco v Stockport MBC* [2003] 4 W.L.R. 1467. However, there is case law to support an action for personal injury in Ireland, *Hanrahan v Merck Sharpe & Dohme* [1998] 1 I.L.R.M. 629.

DEFENCES

As with nuisance (also a strict liability tort) there are a number of defences open to the defendant under the rule in *R v F*.

Act of a Stranger

Where the escape is the result of the unauthorised intervention of a stranger, then the defendant will not be liable for the escape. The only possible liability would be in negligence, for failure to prevent the escape (*Goldman v Hargrave* [1967] 1 A.C. 645).

For instance in *Beutler v Beutler* (1983) 26 C.C.L.T. 229, a drunken driver crashed into a wall damaging a gas meter, causing an escape of gas and an explosion. The gas company in this case was relieved of liability as the escape was due to the act of a third party.

An exception to this general rule is where the defendant is said to control the actions of the "stranger". This would arise in the case of employees, visitors onto property and independent contractors.

Act of God/*Vis Major* (Irresistible Force)

An Act of God or *vis major*, (such as war), will be a good defence to an action in *R v F*. Generally speaking to be an Act of God an occurrence must be the consequence of natural causes exclusively, must be of an extraordinary nature and could not be anticipated or provided against by the defendant (unforeseeable). As such there are very few cases where this defence has been raised successfully.

In the decision in *Superquinn Ltd v Bray UDC*, unreported, High Court, February 18, 1998, Laffoy J. accepted that a hurricane, known as Hurricane Charlie came within "the category of the most extreme natural phenomena ... [and] could not reasonably have been anticipated or guarded against" and constituted an Act of God.

In the case of *Dockeray v Manor Park Homebuilders Ltd*, unreported, High Court, O'Hanlon J., April 10, 1995, however, O'Hanlon J. rejected that an exceptionally heavy rainfall of a kind that happened maybe once every twenty years amounted to an Act of God. This decision lends weight to the principle that only the most extreme natural phenomena will attract this defence.

Statutory Authority

As with nuisance, where a statute authorises a defendant to act in a manner which gives rise to the rule in *R v F*, a defence is afforded to the defendant. Typically this will apply where an escape occurs in the provision of public utilities such as water, gas or electricity.

Consent of the Plaintiff

Where the plaintiff, either expressly or implicitly, consents to the danger the rule of *R v F* will not arise. This is in effect a waiver of the plaintiff's rights. In such cases the only action is one in negligence where this is appropriate. The defence also arises where the danger gives rise to a common benefit, for instance from the use of a gas, electricity or water supply. These cases generally involve a building with multiple occupants where all have consented in some way to the danger. For instance in the case of *Victor Weston (Eire) Ltd v Kenny* [1954] I.R. 191, the flooding of the plaintiff's flat by water used by the building as a whole was deemed to come within the defence of "common benefit" so that the rule in *R v F* did not apply.

14. LIABILITY FOR ANIMALS

INTRODUCTION

Liability for injury caused by animals can be imposed on the basis of the general rules of tort (*Rylands v Fletcher*, nuisance, negligence or trespass) and the special rules (scienter and cattle trespass). A number of legislative provisions have also been introduced which deal with liability for animals (e.g. the Control of Dogs Act 1986 and 1992 and the Animals Act 1985).

Only the special rules and the legislative provisions will be discussed in this chapter but the possibility of founding a case on the existing torts discussed in the other chapters must always be borne in mind. The advantage of founding a case on the special rules rather than relying solely on the general rules is that strict liability may be imposed with the former.

SCIENTER

This refers to the nature of the animal itself. There are two rules, one relating to wild animals and one relating to tame animals. With respect to wild animals (*ferae naturae*) a dangerous nature is presumed and where damage arises, strict liability applies. In the case of tame animals (*mansuetae naturae*) knowledge of a dangerous propensity must be shown before liability will attach. The distinction between tame and wild animals is not always a clear one however, and is generally based on the traits of the species as a whole, rather than on those of individual animals.

Wild Animals

There is no necessity to show that a wild animal has a propensity towards being dangerous, the law assumes that wild animals are naturally dangerous or *ferae naturae*, and this is a presumption that cannot be rebutted. Examples of wild animals would include elephants (*Behrens v Bertram Mills Circus Ltd* [1957] 1 All E.R. 583), bears (*Wyatt v Rosherville Gardens Co* (1886) 2 T.L.R. 282) and zebras (*Marlor v Ball* (1900) 16 T.L.R. 239).

Tame Animals

Strict liability will only apply in relation to tame animals where the owner has knowledge of the dangerous propensity of the animal. Where this criterion is not fulfilled it is for the plaintiff to prove negligence. Examples of tame animals include dogs, cats (*Buckle v Holmes* [1926] 2 K.B. 125) and bees (*O'Gorman v O'Gorman* [1903] 2 I.R. 573).

A dangerous propensity has been described as a vicious, mischievous or fierce tendency, simple playfulness will not be enough. In *Fitzgerald v E.D. and A.D. Cooke Bourne (Farms) Ltd* [1963] 3 W.L.R. 522 the court held that a horse knocking the plaintiff to the ground was not evidence of a dangerous propensity. They held that such behaviour was merely playfulness so no liability was imposed. Similarly, the big playful dog who bounds up to visitors and drools all over them will generally not qualify, however, animals that show a tendency to attack, such as the dog in *Duggan v Armstrong* [1992] I.R. 161, would qualify. McCarthy J. in this case held:

> "One does not have to wait for the growling and frightening dog to bite someone in order to know that it may do so; the requirement of scienter is not that the dog will bite somebody but that, have displayed a vicious propensity, it may do so."

In *Howard v Bergin, O'Connor & Co* [1925] 2 I.R. 110, it was held that the propensity does not have to be permanent. As stated in that case "… what is called a 'mischievous propensity' may be as well a passing or temporary phase of character or temper of the particular animal as a chronic or permanent element of its nature."

Where the tame animal injures another animal no liability will be imposed where the injury is consistent with that animal's "natural instinct". A case in point is that of *Buckle v Holmes* [1926] 2 K.B. 125. The defendant's cat killed 13 pigeons and two bantams owned by the plaintiff. The court distinguished between the injury of humans on the one hand and the injury of other animals on the other. While the former would always constitute evidence of a dangerous propensity, the court held that the latter would only do so where the instinct to injure other animals was not a natural one. As it was natural for the cat to kill pigeons, no dangerous propensity existed.

The defendant must also have knowledge that the animal had a dangerous propensity. The defendant does not have to actually witness the vicious behaviour, if they are told about it that will suffice for actual knowledge. Knowledge which family members or servants hold will also be imputed to the owner. In addition knowledge that a defendant has as to the animal's previous dangerous propensity will satisfy the requirement of present knowledge. In *Quinn v Quinn* 39 I.L.T.R. 163, for instance, the court held that the defendant's knowledge that a sow had attacked and killed fowl in the past was sufficient to prove the past propensity and to make the defendant liable for the sow now attacking and killing the plaintiff's cow.

CATTLE TRESPASS

Cattle trespass is one of the most ancient causes of action known to the common law and is a somewhat complicated rule. It imposes strict liability where cattle stray of their own violation from land on which they were originally kept, onto the land of another and cause damage, provided that they arrived onto that land either directly or via the highway. If on the other hand, they are driven onto someone else's property the rules of trespass only will apply. Alternatively, in a case where they are brought onto the highway and then stray onto someone's land, negligence rules apply. The rule that cattle lawfully on the highway who stray onto another's land is not covered by cattle trespass, has been defended on the ground of volenti, i.e. that by having land adjoining the highway the plaintiff in some way, accepts the risk that animals will stray onto it.

Cattle for the purposes of this rule includes the bovine variety, however, the term is broader than just this and includes horses, sheep, goats, pigs and in the case of *Brady v Warren* [1900] 2 I.R. 632 it was held that domestic deer could be cattle. On the other hand cats, dogs and wild animals will not constitute cattle.

If the plaintiff wishes to take an action for cattle trespass, it should be taken against the person who has control or possession over the animals, the ownership of the property is less of an issue. In *Dalton v O'Sullivan* [1947] Ir. Jur. Rep. 25, for instance, the case against the owner of cattle, which caused damage when they strayed from land, failed. It was held in this case that the owner who lived 100 miles away and who neither owned the land or tended the cattle, did not have possession of them and could not be liable. The case ought to have been taking against the person tending the animals (see also *Winters v Owens* [1950] I.R. 22.)

The right of action appears to rest in the occupier of land only, and not to others who may be on the land and it has been held that the plaintiff can recover for any damage done to the land, crops and animals on the land. It was also established in the case of *Wormald v Cole* [1954] 1 All E.R. 683 that recovery for personal injuries was also possible. In this case a woman of about 80 years of age was knocked down and injured by a heifer that had strayed onto her land. The defendant argued that recovery for personal injuries was not a feature of the tort of cattle trespass. It was accepted by the Court of Appeal that while originally the damage in an action of cattle trespass was confined to damage to the surface trespassed on and to the depasturing of the crop, there was no reason that it ought not cover personal injuries also.

Defences to Cattle Trespass

A defendant will be able to escape liability for cattle trespass where they can show that the reason for the trespass was the fault of the plaintiff, or an Act of God or the act of a third party as in *Moloney v Stephens* [1945] Ir. Jur. Rep. 37. In this case the defendant succeeded in proving that a third party left the defendant's gate open so that his cattle strayed onto the plaintiff's property.

LEGISLATION

In addition to the special rules of scienter above, there are a number of pieces of legislation that govern liability for animals.

Control of Dogs Act 1986 and 1992

The Control of Dogs Acts are important in that they impose strict liability for any injuries caused by a dog that either attacks a person or causes injury to livestock (s.21(1) of the 1986 Act). It will no longer be necessary to show the existence of a previous mischievous propensity or to show in the alternative that the owner of a dog was negligent.

There are however, two exceptions to this general rule. The first arises in the case of injury to livestock that stray onto land. In this case a person will not be liable unless they have caused the dog to attack (s.21(2)). If this is not the case the principles of scienter must be applied to determine liability. An additional exception exists where the injured person is a trespasser onto land (s.21(3)). The person who keeps the dog on the premises in the event of an injury to a trespasser will only be liable if it can be shown that they were negligent.

Section 21(1) requires an attack on a person (but mere injury to livestock) for strict liability to apply. An attack in this case seems to require directness (a dog must attack the person and not their car for instance) and also intend injury.

Section 21(4) states that the provisions of the Civil Liability Act 1961 also apply, which means that provisions with respect to contributory negligence, concurrent wrongdoers and fatal injuries are all covered by this Act, also the time limitations that run for personal injuries will run here also.

Animals Act 1985

The Animals Act 1985 was introduced to reform an old common law immunity which provided that the owner of an animal that strayed onto the highway was not liable for damage caused by that animal. The rule was developed in the case of *Searle v Wallbank* [1947] A.C. 341 and was applied in a number of Irish cases such as *Dunphy v Bryan* (1963) I.L.T.R. 4.

Following pressure for reform the immunity was removed by the 1985 Act. Section 2 of the Animals Act provides that the principles of negligence must be applied to determine such cases in the future. Generally speaking, if an injured party could show that fencing was defective then this would be enough to prove a lack of reasonable care. If however, the area was one where fencing was not customary, the absence of fencing alone will not amount to negligence.

Cases of animals escaping onto the highway are also characteristic of cases which attract the principle of *res ipsa loquitur* (see Chapter 3). As stated in *O'Reilly v Lavelle* [1990] 2 I.R. 372 "Cattle properly managed should not stray onto the road … I believe that there is no matter more appropriate for the application of the doctrine of res ipsa loquitur than cattle wandering on the highway." See also *O'Shea v Tilman Anhold and Horse Holiday Farm Ltd*, unreported, Supreme Court, Hamilton C.J., O'Flaherty, Keane JJ., October 23, 1996.

15. DEFAMATION

INTRODUCTION

The tort of defamation seeks to strike a balance between a person's right to the protection of his or her good name and reputation on the one hand and the right to freely express views and opinions on the other. These rights are also protected by the Irish Constitution (Art.40.3.2 and Art. 40.6.1.ii.) and the European Convention on Human Rights (ECHR), which protects both freedom of expression (art.10) and a person's right to privacy (art.8). While the tort of defamation applies to all utterances, in practice the vast majority of cases are taken against the media.

The Defamation Act 2009 (the Act) was enacted on July 23, 2009, bringing about the most significant reform of the law of defamation in Ireland in almost 40 years. It repeals the earlier Defamation Act 1961 (which had regulated the law to a certain extent) and radically alters the common law position bringing it into line with obligations under the ECHR. The Act follows from a number of reports in recent years, most significantly the Law Reform Commission Report on the Civil Law of Defamation in 1991 and the Report of the Legal Advisory Group on Defamation 2003. At the time of writing (July 2009) the Act has not been commenced but it expected that a Commencement Order will be signed by the Minister for Justice commencing the Act in its entirety in the coming months.

A Privacy Bill was also introduced in 2006 but the progress of this Bill has been much slower. It was intended however, that both pieces of legislation would work in tandem to protect both the right to free speech and the right to privacy.

This chapter will discuss the tort of defamation only. The Defamation Act 2009 is not retrospective (s.3(1)) so the pre-Act position will apply to any actions arising before the commencement of the Act. The Act also does not affect the "general law" in relation to defamation unless the Act deals specifically with it (s.3(2)).

DEFINITION

The Defamation Act 2009 gives a statutory definition to defamation for the first time. Section 6(2) states that:

"The tort of defamation consists of the publication, by any means, of a defamatory statement concerning a person to one or more than one person (other than the first-mentioned person), and "defamation" shall be construed accordingly."

Section 2 of the Act defines a defamatory statement and states that,

"… 'defamatory statement' means a statement that tends to injure a person's reputation in the eyes of reasonable members of society, and 'defamatory' shall be construed accordingly."

This replaces the common law definition of defamation, enunciated by Walsh J. in *Quigley v Creation Ltd* [1971] I.R. 269 (in turn drawn from that provided by Lord Aiken in *Sin v Stretch* [1936] 2 All E.R. 1237) which stated that defamation consisted of:

"The wrongful publication of a false statement about a person, which tends to lower that person in the eyes of right-thinking members of society or tends to hold that person up to hatred, ridicule or contempt, or causes that person to be shunned or avoided by right-thinking members of society."

As can be noted from the statutory definition, the "right-thinking members" of society have now been replaced by "reasonable members" of society (recommended by the Law Reform Commission Report on Defamation 1991) and arguably strikes less of a moral tone. Curiously, the definition does not specify that the statement must be "false" or "untrue" but as "truth" is retained as a defence in s.14 of the Act the practical effect is that any "true" statement will not be defamatory if the truth of the statement can be shown.

Liability attaches to a statement which "tends" to injure a person's reputation, there is no necessity to prove harm, reflecting the common law view that damage is presumed to flow from a defamatory statement.

PUBLICATION

Before a statement can be defamatory it must be published. Section 2 of the Act defines statements broadly as including statements made orally or in writing, visual images, sounds, gestures or any other method of signifying meaning, including statements broadcast on radio or television, published on the internet or by electronic communication.

This reflects the earlier position as defined in s.14(2) of the Defamation Act 1961 which stated that publication of words included "reference to visual images, gestures and other methods of signifying meaning."

As stated above s.6(2) of the Act requires that publication be made to a third party. So shouting something potentially defamatory to an empty room or communicating privately to the plaintiff will not constitute defamation. The position between married couples prior to the Act was that communication between spouses did not constitute publication as they were viewed as one unit. The more modern view is that given the high public policy value placed on privacy between spouses such communications attract absolute privilege (see below). The Act itself is silent at to communications between spouses but as s.14 of the Act states that any communications attracting "absolute privilege" prior to the Act's enactment continue to do so after the fact, then such communications should continue to enjoy this status. Otherwise the position relating to spouses will no doubt remain in any event by virtue of s.3(2).

Accidental Communication

Where publication is unintended or accidental a person can still be liable if the publication was foreseen. In *Paul v Holt* (1935) 69 I.L.T. 157 the plaintiff owed the defendant arrears in rent. He sent a letter addressed to Mr Paul, with no first name specified. It happened that the plaintiff lived with his brother, also a Mr Paul, who opened the letter. This was held to be sufficient publication to lead to liability. Evidence was submitted that the defendant knew that the plaintiff lived with his brother. However, where a person opens a letter without authorisation this will not amount to publication.

Section 6(4) of the Act also provides a defence in the event of unintended and unforeseeable publication, where the publication was made to the person to whom it relates and a third party. The defence will apply where the publication was not intended to be seen by the third party and it was not reasonably foreseeable that it would be seen. This is very similar to the situation in *Paul* above but as publication in that case was reasonably foreseeable, the defence in s.6(4) would not have applied.

WHO CAN BE SUED FOR PUBLICATION?

A wide range of people can be sued for defamation if they have been in any way involved in its publication. The initial communicator, as well as other distributors such as publishers, printers, retailers, and the media can all be sued. In the event of a person making multiple publications, the position prior to the Act had been that an action could be taken for each publication. Section 11 of the Act now provides than in respect of multiple publications by a defendant an action may only be taken against that person once unless "the interests of justice so require" in which case the court can give leave to more than one action to be taken.

Prior to the Act an exception to the general principle of liability for publication was available to distributors, (other than the original publisher, media and printers) who could show that:

- They had no knowledge of the defamatory content of the material;
- Nothing in material or surrounding circumstances gave them grounds to suspect any defamatory content; and
- They were not negligent in failing to discover the defamatory content.

The onus was on the defendant to show that this is the case.

This defence has been extended and modified by s.27 of the Act and renamed the defence of "Innocent Publication". The defence now applies to anyone other than the original author, editor or publisher who can show that they took reasonable care in the publication of the statement, and had no reason to believe that what they did contributed to or caused the publication of a defamatory statement. Included in the category of those who can avail of the defence are those who were the printers, distributors or broadcasters of defamatory material. In this way, television and radio broadcasters are included as are those who distribute or show films. It will be particularly useful in the case of live broadcasts or radio shows, but contingent on reasonable care being taken.

TYPES OF PUBLICATION

Prior to the Act defamation could take the form of slander or libel. This distinction has been abolished by the Act and replaced by a single tort of defamation (s.6(1)). There will no longer be a necessity to show "special damage" when suing for the tort of defamation regardless of the form the publication takes (s.6(5)).

Libel/Slander Distinction

Generally speaking a libel is a communication in a permanent or lasting form, such as the written word. Slander is defamation by communication in a transient form, such as spoken words. Interestingly, although live broadcasts are spoken they were considered a permanent form of communication and were therefore a libel (s.15 of the Defamation Act 1961.) A written statement which is read out was also a libel (reflecting the principle of "once a libel, always a libel"). The distinction existed as it was presumed that not only has more thought and deliberation gone into the making a written statement, but also that as it is in a permanent form it can do more damage.

There were two important distinctions between the torts of libel and slander. Firstly, a libel was a crime as well as a tort and as such could be subject to criminal proceedings (see Pt III of the Defamation Act 1961). Libel also was actionable per se (you did not have to show damage) whereas only some forms of slander were actionable without showing special damage.

The slanders which were actionable per se were as follows:

i.   Words (including images, gestures or other methods of signifying meaning), which impute unchastity or adultery to any woman or girl (s.16 of Defamation Act 1961). An argument could be made of course that this is unconstitutional on the basis that it offends principles of equality (Art.40.1).
ii. Slanders affecting a person's official, professional or business reputation (s.19 of the Defamation Act).
iii. Slanders imputing a criminal offence punishable by death or imprisonment.
iv. Slanders imputing a contagious disease which tends to exclude the sufferer from society.

If the slander did not fall into one of the four categories referred to above the plaintiff would have to show special damage. Special damage in this context required material damage of some sort, such as loss of business, loss or refusal of an office or employment, the dismissal from a situation or the loss of a client. Loss of reputation without some material loss would not suffice (*Dinnegan v Ryan*, unreported, High Court, Murray J., May 13, 2002). As discussed above the distinction between libel and slander has been established by s.6(1) of the Act.

DEFAMATORY

The Act requires that the publication must be false (in that the "truth" of the statement will act as a defence) and must be capable of lowering a person's reputation in the eyes of "reasonable members of society". The pre-Act position was that the statement had to be capable of lowering the person in the eyes of right-thinking members of society, or of holding them up to hatred, ridicule or contempt, or be capable of causing that person to be shunned or avoided by right-thinking members of society. In determining whether a statement is defamatory, the judge, or in the High Court if sitting with a jury, the jury, seeks to reflect the views of society. As the views of society change over time, determining whether a publication is defamatory is a highly unpredictable exercise.

Standard

The standard is an objective one, concerned not with the plaintiff's intention but rather with the impact the publication will generate in the mind of others. It is important to note that no adverse effect needs to be shown, it is enough to show that the publication had the propensity to have an adverse effect on a person's reputation. A publication may be defamatory given the word's ordinary and natural meaning, or it may be defamatory as a result of innuendo (what the statements suggest).

In cases involving publications which relate to an individual's moral character the courts have handed down a number of revealing judgments. In the case of *Youssoupoff v Metro-Goldwyn-Mayer Pictures Ltd* (1934) 50 Times L.R. 581 it was held that to say that a woman was raped would be defamatory to her character. The case involved a film made about the life of Rasputin that implied that the plaintiff, Princess Youssoupoff, had been raped. Scrutton L.J., in finding for the plaintiff held that the libel was "the vilest possible libel on a woman", and on appeal Slesser L.J. called the implication an "exceedingly grave libel on this lady." These comments were reiterated in the *Quigley* case almost 40 years later, when Walsh J., stated that:

"In a community which places a high value on female chastity, to say untruthfully that she was a victim of rape may well lower her in the eyes of the community by creating an undesirable interest in her or by leaving her exposed to the risk of being shunned or avoided ...".

In the case of *Reynolds v Malocco t/a "Patrick"* [1999] 2 I.R. 203 it was held that to imply that someone was a homosexual was also defamatory. The plaintiff argued that many people in Ireland could see it as a form of sexual deviancy and the court agreed. However, given the changing nature of societal mores it is difficult to say whether courts would find the same today.

Generally speaking any publication that prejudices an individual's professional character or calls into question their competence or honesty in their trade or profession is defamatory. This includes of course politicians. In the case of *De Rossa v Independent Newspapers Plc* [1999] 4 I.R. 432, the Supreme Court upheld an award to the plaintiff of £300,000 arising from an article written by Eamon Dunphy in the Irish Independent newspaper. The article alleged that funding for Democratic Left, the party of which the plaintiff was a leader, came from criminal sources and implied that the leader had knowledge of such. This was held to be defamatory of the plaintiff's political reputation. Given the political climate in Ireland in relation to Northern Ireland it was at one time unclear whether it would be defamatory of a person's character to allege that they possessed republican sympathies. In *Berry v Irish Times Ltd* [1973] I.R. 368, such an allegation was made. The plaintiff, then secretary of the Department of Justice, brought a case against the Irish Times for publication of a picture of a person holding a placard which stated, "Peter Berry—20th Century Felon Setter—Helped Jail Republicans in England." The jury found that the words were not defamatory and this finding was upheld by the Supreme Court. Ó Dálaigh J. held that:

"To say that ... such an allegation must be defamatory would be to hold that ordinary right-thinking people on this country could not condemn such militant activities ... but think that a person who assisted in curbing or putting down such militant activities was guilty of disgraceful conduct."

However, two dissenting judgments highlighted the difficulty in reaching a decision in that case. The dissenting judges held that the allegation that the plaintiff had acted as a spy and informer for the British police concerning republicans in England put the plaintiff into the same category as the spies and informer of earlier centuries who were regarded with "loathing and abomination by all decent people."

It is clear that in today's political climate that such allegations would not constitute defamation (see *McDonagh v News Group Newspapers Ltd*, unreported, Supreme Court, November 23, 1993.)

INNUENDO

A statement can be defamatory on the basis of the ordinary and natural meaning given to those words, or on the basis of "reading between the lines" or otherwise put, innuendo. Innuendo may be a "false innuendo", where the defamatory meaning can be understood from the words without further information, or the innuendo may be a "true (or legal) innuendo" where additional knowledge is required for the defamatory meaning to be appreciated. It is immaterial to the success of an action for "true innuendo" whether the public in general has access to the additional information required.

False Innuendo

In the case of *Reynolds v Malocco t/a "Patrick"* [1999] 2 I.R. 203, the plaintiff was a nightclub owner in Dublin. He objected to the publication of an article in which it was implied that he was gay and engaged in criminal activities. Despite the fact that there was no clear statement of either allegation the court held that there was sufficient innuendo to this effect to constitute defamation.

Legal or true Innuendo

Where the plaintiff claims legal innuendo he or she must prove the additional facts which make the statement defamatory. In *Tolley v Fry & Sons Ltd* [1931] A.C. 333 for instance, the plaintiff, an amateur golfer, was pictured with a packet of the defendant's chocolate, as a way of advertising the chocolate. Although the words taken in their natural and ordinary meaning were not defamatory, when one added the additional fact the plaintiff was an amateur sportsman it implied that he had sold his reputation for advertising purposes, contrary to the spirit of amateurism. He succeeded in his defamation action.

IDENTIFICATION OF THE PLAINTIFF

In order for a defamation action to succeed the plaintiff must be identified. In some cases it will be clear that the person referred to is the plaintiff, in that he or she may be named specifically, and an address, or picture, or other description may be given. However, in other cases it may not be clear, in which case the question arises as to what will amount to sufficient identification. In *Knupffer v London Express Newspaper Ltd* [1944] A.C. 116 the test in such cases was described as follows:

> "Where the plaintiff is not named, the test which decides whether the words used refer to him is the question whether the words are such as would reasonably lead persons acquainted with the plaintiff to believe that he was the person referred to" (approved in *Duffy v News Group Newspapers Ltd* [1994] 3 I.R. 63).

This principle is reflected in s.6(3) of the Act which states that "A defamatory statement concerns a person if it could reasonably be understood as referring to him or her."

Reference to a Class

If reference is made to a class or group of people and not an individual then again it is for the plaintiff to demonstrate that the publication could be reasonably held to refer to him or her. Needless to say it is easier to achieve with a small group as opposed to a large one.

Section 10 of the Act now states that where a defamatory statement is made about a class of persons, a member of that class will have an action if:

> "*(a)* by reason of the number of persons who are members of that class, or
> *(b)* by virtue of the circumstances in which the statement is published,
> the statement could reasonably be understood to refer, in particular, to the member concerned."

DEFENCES

Given the struggle between the competing interests of free expression and the right to a good name, it is not surprising that a number of defences have emerged. These are deemed to be vital in a democratic society to safeguard the interests served by allowing open and honest criticism of public figures without being open to a threat of legal action. Section 15 of the Act repeals all of the former defences, except statutory defences or defences available pursuant to European Law. Notwithstanding s.15, the defences available in the Act are largely reflective of the pre-Act position. A significant addition to the category of available defences is the defence of "Fair and reasonable publication on a matter of public interest" which is an entirely new defence aimed primarily to facilitate the media in its reporting on public figures. The defences are discussed below.

Justification/Truth

The defence of justification is a valid and complete defence if the defendant can prove that the defamatory statement is substantially true, even if it is not true in every detail. As a defamatory statement is presumed to be false, it rests with the defendant to prove that the statement is true if he wishes to rely on this defence. The defence has been renamed the defence of "Truth" in s.16 of the Act but it otherwise largely reflects the pre-Act position.

As stated in the Act the defence shall apply if the defendant can show that the statement is true "in all material respects". Section 16(2) of the Act further qualifies the defence by stating that that where two distinct charges are made against the plaintiff, the defence of justification will still apply even though the defendant cannot prove each one. This applies so long as the ones not proven do not cause any additional damage to the plaintiff's reputation given the damage done by the ones proven to be true—this reflects the former provision in s.22 of the Defamation Act 1961. The operation of the principle can be seen in a number of cases. In *Crawford v Todd* (1941) 75 I.L.T.R. 233 it was stated that the defendant kept a "Hell's gambling den" and that he sold intoxicating liquor without a licence. The defendant could not prove the truth of the second allegation and as they were seen as "distinct charges" the defence failed. On the other hand in the case of *Cooper-Flynn v RTE* [2000] 3 I.R. 344, the defence of justification succeeded. The plaintiff had been accused of advising or encouraging a Mr Howard (the third defendant) and other unnamed investors to participate in an investment scheme which had as its purpose the evasion of tax liabilities. While the jury did not accept that she had encouraged Mr Howard to evade his taxes they did accept that she had encouraged others, in this way the statement made was deemed to be substantially true and therefore not defamatory of her character.

Privilege

The defence of privilege can be pleaded in specific cases where the statement made is protected as it is in the public interest to allow uninhibited expression in certain cases.

There are two types of privilege:

(i) Absolute privilege, where the defendant is totally protected in respect of any statements which he may make irrespective of motive or knowledge;
(ii) Qualified privilege, where the defendant is protected except where the statement has been made maliciously.

Absolute Privilege

Section 17(1) of the Act states that any publication which attracted the defence of absolute privilege prior to the commencement of the Act will continue to do so. Section 17(2) lists the incidences in which the Act confers the defence, these are largely reflective of the pre-Act position. The communications which attract absolute privilege are as follows:

• Parliamentary privilege:
This extends to any comments made in either House of the Oireachtas and to any official reports and publications (Arts.15.12 and 15.13 of the Constitution). A legislative provision, s.2 of the Committees of the Houses of the Oireachtas (Privilege and Procedure) Act 1976, extends this immunity to committees of the Oireachtas when the statements are made by members of either house, or by the advisers, officials and agents of such committees, or by witnesses before such committees (see also s.17(2)(l)). This immunity also applies to the documents and reports of such committees. The defence further applies to statements made in the European Parliament, to reports of such statements and to statements made in committees of the European Parliament.

• Judicial proceedings:
Statements made during judicial proceedings, or in preparation of a trial, or in documents and pleadings connected to proceedings made by

judges, counsel, witnesses, solicitors or parties to the proceedings are absolutely privileged. Included are proceedings in the Irish courts, international courts, tribunals established by law, commissions of inquiry, coroner inquests, inquiries (in the Republic or in Northern Ireland) established by the Government, Houses of the Oireachtas, or a court and reports of such inquiries. The statement made must be in connection with the trial and must not go beyond its remit. In *Desmond and MCD Management Services Ltd v Riordan* [2000] 1 I.L.R.M. 502, it was stated that "Once [the judge] is aware of the fact that he is exceeding his jurisdiction and continues to act then in my view he automatically ceases to be administering the law and the need for the immunity ceases." In this case the person found to have gone beyond the scope of his immunity was the coroner who gave evidence in the trial.

Witnesses also may lose their absolute privilege if they exceed the scope of their immunity. As stated in *Re Haughey* [1917] I.R. 217,

> "… if a witness were to take advantage of his position to utter something defamatory having no reference to the cause of matter of inquiry but introduced maliciously for his own purpose, no privilege or immunity would attach and he might find himself sued in an action for defamation."

• Presidential privilege:
This privilege is bases on a Constitutional provision (Art.13.8.1) which states that,

> "The President shall not be answerable to either House of the Oireachtas or to any court for the exercise and performance of the powers and functions of his office."

Therefore the President can never be sued for anything said in his or her capacity as President and connected with the functions of the office of the President.

At common law the fair and accurate reporting of judicial proceedings is privileged, it is not confined to the media, and is not restricted to contemporaneous reports. Section 17(2)(i)–(k) of the Act reflects this defence, which applies provided that the report made is fair and accurate and that the judicial proceeding was heard in public. The reported statement must have formed part of the proceedings, and not simply have been the utterances of a bystander in the court (*Lynam v Gowing* (1880) 6 L. R. Ir. 259).

• State communications:
Communications between the Executive and the President and between members of the Executive on business pertaining to their functions are absolutely privileged.

Qualified Privilege

The defence of qualified privileged is available where for the common good it is felt that uninhibited expression should be allowed. This would arise where for instance someone suspects a crime is being committed and contacts the police, or a person wishes to make a complaint and contacts the relevant body. In either case the person may be incorrect, but ought their publication give rise to an action in defamation? The courts have held that it ought not, provided the person who uttered the statement has a duty to do so, the person to whom it is communicated had an interest in receiving it and the making of the statement was free from malice.

Section 18 of the Act retains this defence and states that the defence will apply where the defendant can prove that the person who receives it has a duty or interest in receiving it and that the defendant believed upon reasonable grounds that the person had such a duty or interest. Section 19 of the Act states that the defence will fail if the plaintiff can prove that the defendant acted with malice.

Duty

The duty to communicate a statement may be a legal, moral or social one. In *Hartery v Welltrade (Middle East) Ltd and Hurley* [1978] I.L.R.M. 38 a complaint was made to the police and the Law Society of a possible blackmail. Although the complaint was based on a misunderstanding and was incorrect it was held to attract the defence of qualified privilege. It was reasonable and the defendants clearly felt they had a duty to report it.

In cases where the statement is made by way of a moral or social duty the courts look more favourably on cases where the publication was requested rather than volunteered. For instance in *Gillis v M'Donnell* (1869) I.R. 4 C.L. 342, a volunteered communication between strangers was held not to have been privileged.

Interest

The statement made must be made to a person, group or organisation that has an interest in receiving it. In the *Hartery* case above the complaint of blackmailing was made to the appropriate parties, i.e. the Law Society and the Gardaí. The Act will also protect those however who have reasonable grounds for believing that the person or body has an interest in receiving it. Section 18(2)(a)(ii) states that it will be a defence for a defendant to prove that they had reasonable grounds for believing that the person to whom they communicated a defamatory statement had a duty or interest in receiving it and s.18(2) states that the defence of qualified privilege will not fail simply because the defendant mistook the party to whom the statement was communicated as an interested party. The law prior to the Act did not protect statements where the publisher had made a mistake in relation to the appropriateness of the receiving body. In the case of *Hynes-O'Sullivan v O'Driscoll* [1989] I.L.R.M. 349 the defendant failed to identify the correct organisation and could not rely on the defence of qualified privilege. In this case the defendant, a solicitor, accused the plaintiff who was a witness in one of his cases, of "duplicity" and described her as a person "who holds scant regard for professional ethics and even less for the solemnity of the law." The defendant sent a copy of this letter to the Irish Medical Association with a covering letter making a formal complaint against the plaintiff. Unfortunately for the defendant the correct body to whom the complaint ought to have been made was the Irish Medical Council. On the question of whether reasonable belief of the appropriateness of the body was sufficient Finlay C.J. held that it was not, stating that "… I take the view that a mere honest belief in the appropriateness of recipient is not sufficient under any circumstances to create privilege …". Once the Act has been commenced this will not longer be the case and such communications will be protected.

Malice Destroying Qualified Privilege

Despite the fact that the duty and interest tests may be satisfied, a statement may lose the right to claim qualified privilege as a defence if that statement was made with malice. Malice was described in the case of *Clarke v Molyneaux* (1877) 3 QBD 246 as a statement made for an indirect or wrong motive, with reckless disregard as to the truth of the statement.

Reports

Section 24 of the Defamation Act 1961 also protected publication in newspapers or in the broadcast media of a wide range of reports as set out in the second schedule. They included fair and accurate reporting of any proceedings in public of a house of the legislature of any foreign state or international organisation (or conference) of which Ireland is a member (or to which Ireland sends a representative). Reporting on the proceedings of any foreign or international court, the fair and accurate copies or extracts from a public register or reporting of notices or advertisements of courts in the State or in Northern Ireland were also included.

Statements privileged subject to explanation (if requested by the plaintiff) included fair and accurate reports of the findings or decisions of associations (or their committees) promoting art, science, religion or learning, trade, business, industrial or professional associations or sporting associations.

This is retained in the Act where s.18(3) and s.18(4) state that publications relating to matters outlined in Pt 1 of Sch.1 and Pt 2 of Sch.1 are privileged.

Fair Comment/Defence of Honest Opinion

Publications made in good faith on a matter of public interest are protected by the defence traditionally known as the defence of fair comment. In *London Artists v Littler* [1969] 2 Q.B. 375 the court described when the defence could apply as follows:

> "Whether a matter is such as it will affect people at large, so that they may be legitimately interested in, or concerned at, what is going on; or what may happen to them or others; then it is a matter of public interest on which everyone is entitled to make fair comment."

The Act has renamed this defence the defence of "honest opinion". Section 20 states that the defence will apply to statements of opinion relating to a matter of public interest where the defendant can prove that the opinion was honestly held. Section 20(2) states that an opinion will be "honest" where:

(a) the defendant can show that the author believed in the truth of the statement and the opinion was based on facts specified in the

publication or referred to in the publication and of general
knowledge. The defendant will also have to prove the truth of the
allegations of fact on which the opinion has been based, or

(b)   the defendant can show that they are based on allegations of fact
to which the defence of qualified privilege or absolute privilege
would apply. Again the defendant will have to prove the truth of
these allegations, or else that he or she could not have known that
the allegations were untrue or that the opinion published could
not reasonably lead a person to understand that the allegations
were true.

Generally speaking any matter relating to the government or the
administration of the State, or any matter of a literary, artistic, or
similar nature, will be a matter of public interest. It is important that the
opinion must be based on facts which are stated or otherwise widely
known or the defence may fail. In *Foley v Independent Newspapers
(Ireland) Ltd* [1994] 2 I.L.R.M. 61 an inspector was appointed to
investigate certain matters under the Companies Act 1990 and was
criticised by the defendants as having charged exorbitant fees. The
defence of fair comment failed as they had omitted from their article
the fact that the fees had been negotiated in advance with the State.

Offer to make Amends

Section 21 of the Defamation Act 1961 provided that if an offer of
amends was made (by way of retraction or correction for instance) as
soon as practicable after a defamatory statement was made, and the
defendant could show that the publication had been innocent and not
unreasonable, this would afford a complete defence to the defendant.

Section 22 of the Act retains this defence. The offer must be made
prior to any defence in a defamation action being delivered; it must be
in writing and it must explain the nature and scope of the offer. An
"offer to make amends" is described in s.22(5) as a personal correction
and apology to the person concerned, a published correction and
apology and a payment of compensation and/or costs. Section 23(3)
provides that where the offer is rejected, the making of such an offer
will constitute a complete defence. This will apply unless the plaintiff
can prove that the defendant made the defamatory statement knowing
that it referred to the plaintiff and was false and defamatory or that the
defendant ought reasonably to have known that this was the case.

Apology

An apology is not a defence in a traditional sense but if made before the commencement of an action or as soon as practicable afterwards, it will be admissible in mitigation of damages. Section 24 of the Act is worded in similar terms to s.17 of the Defamation Act 1961, which stated that apology may be relevant in "mitigation of damage". The apology must be given the same or similar prominence in any publication or an offer to do so must be made. The Act also states that an apology will not constitute an admission of liability nor can it be used in any civil proceedings against the defendant (ss.24(3) and (4)).

Consent

A person cannot bring an action in defamation if he or she has consented to the publication of the offending statement under contract. Likewise a person cannot complain if they have agreed to waive their legal rights in respect of it, whether or not for value. Section 25 of the Act retains this as a defence.

Fair and Reasonable Publication on a Matter of Public Interest

Section 26 of the Act introduces a new defence called the defence of "fair and reasonable publication on a matter of public interest". It was introduced in response to the difficulties faced by the media in particular in reporting on the activities of public figures (such reporting generally seen as being in the public interest) but who could not easily rely on any of the other established defences. The defence of qualified privilege for instance did not apply in most cases to such publications as it was held that the public was too wide a group to possess sufficient "interest" in receiving a statement. For that reason the defence has not generally been open to media reports directed at the public. Despite this general rule, there is a degree of leniency given in most jurisdictions regarding statements made about political figures, in particular by the media. In the case of *New York Times v Sullivan* (1964) 376 US 254 the US courts held that where the media publish false statements about public figures there will be no defamation provided that the statement is made without malice. This has been echoed in New Zealand in the case of *Lange v Atkinson and Australian Consolidated Press NZ Ltd* [1998] 3 N.Z.L.R. 424, where false statements about political figures to the public at large are protected provided that the publication is not motivated by ill-will. In Australia also such publications attract the defence of qualified privilege provided that reasonable care is used in the making of such statements. No such definitive decisions have been given in this jurisdiction. Generally speaking, statements made about political figures made to the public do not attract any defence other than that of fair comment or justification. In the case of *Reynolds v Times Newspapers Ltd* [1999] 4 All E.R. 609 however, the defendants tried to argue that such statements should automatically attract the defence of qualified privilege, introducing a position akin to that in the US and New Zealand. The House of Lords rejected that "political information" ought to automatically attract the defence but accepted that it could do so when all circumstances were considered. These were described by Lord Nicholls as follows: the seriousness of the allegations; the nature of the information; the source of the information; steps taken to verify the information; status of the information; urgency of the matter; whether comment was sought from the plaintiff; tone of the article; circumstances of publication. In the *Reynolds* case, as the defendants had not included the plaintiff's side of the story, they did not benefit from the defence of qualified privilege. In *Gerry Hunter v Gerald Duckworth and Company Ltd, Louis Blom Cooper*, unreported, High Court, July, 2003 O'Caoimh J. approved the judgment in *Reynolds* and stated that in the absence of legislative provisions, the best person to decide whether a publication to the public at large should enjoy qualified privilege was the judge in any particular case.

Following from this background s.26 of the Act has been introduced to protect statements made in good faith, on a matter of public interest, the discussion of which is for the benefit of the public. The publication must be fair and reasonable. Section 26(2) outlines the considerations in deciding whether a publication will be deemed to be "fair and reasonable" and they include many of the considerations described in *Reynolds* including whether they related to a person's public duties, the seriousness, context and content of the allegations, adherence to code of standards of the Press Council, membership of the Press Council and steps taken to establish the accuracy of what was being published including representing the plaintiff's version of events.

REMEDIES

The Act provides for the following remedies: a declaratory order (s.28)); lodgment of money in settlement of an action (without admission of liability) s.29; a correction order (s.30); damages (ss.31 and 32); an order prohibiting the publication of a defamatory statement (s.33). The Act also allows for the summary disposal of an action in favour of either the plaintiff or a defendant (s.34).

DAMAGES

Damages in a defamation action are decided by the "court" which means the judge or for actions taken in the High Court when sitting with a jury, the jury (s.31(3) of the Act). In the High Court, which sits with a jury in defamation actions, the position prior to the Act was that the jury assessed damages without any guidance from the judge (see *De Rossa v Independent Newspapers Plc* [1999] 4 I.R. 432 where £300,000 was awarded, and *O'Brien v Mirror Group Newspapers Ltd* [2001] I.R. 1 where £250,000 was awarded). Section 31 of the Act now amends this position and allows parties to a defamation action to make submissions to the court in relation to damages and further allows a judge to give directions to a jury where applicable. An assessment as to damages will be made by the court having regard to "all the circumstances of the case" (s.31(3)). In addition s.31(4) lists a number of factors which the court must take into account, including the nature, gravity and extent of the defamatory statement, the reputation of the person defamed, and attempts to make amends by the publisher of the statement. The Act also brings about a substantial change to the position in relation to appeals to the Supreme Court on the issue of damages. Prior to the Act the Supreme Court could, where it deemed appropriate, refer a case back to the High Court for a reassessment on the issue of damages, but it did not substitute its own award for that of the High Court. Section 13 of the Act amends this position, stating that: "Upon the hearing of an appeal from a decision of the High Court in a defamation action, the Supreme Court may, in addition to any other order that it deems appropriate to make, substitute for any amount of damages awarded to the plaintiff by the High Court such amount as it considers appropriate."

16. REMEDIES

INTRODUCTION

There are principally three types of remedies available to a claimant in a tort action. One is the legal remedy of damages. Legal remedies are available, as of right, once the tort is proven. The second is the equitable remedy of an injunction. Equitable remedies are by their nature discretionary, i.e. it is up to the court to decide in any particular case if it is reasonable to provide an equitable remedy. While damages are often the most appropriate remedy, in some cases, such as that of nuisance, an injunction may also be awarded. Both of these remedies are available through the courts. Damages are also available by way of application to the InjuiresBoard.ie (see Chapter 1). The third remedy is that of "self-help" i.e. where the plaintiff takes action to remedy the wrong. This can arise in cases of trespass for instance, where the plaintiff can take reasonable steps to prevent injury to person or to land. Similarly with nuisance cases the plaintiff can take reasonable steps to abate the nuisance. This third remedy is discussed in this book under the relevant torts where appropriate. It is worth however bearing in mind that as with all self-help steps taken by the plaintiff, the underlying principle is that the action must be reasonable.

DAMAGES

The principle underlying all awards of damages is that of *restitutio in intergrum*, which is to restore the person to the position they would have been in had the tort not arisen. Clearly in some cases where the loss is not a financial one this is impossible. If a leg is lost for instance a monetary award will not restore it to the plaintiff, but in the view of the court such an award will at least compensate to some degree for the loss suffered.

Damages are awarded as a lump sum. The advantage of such a practice is that the matter is then disposed of. The disadvantage however is that the method of calculating future loss becomes a complicated accounting exercise.

If the case is taken to court the decision as to the level of the award is in almost all cases, taken by a judge. Juries were at one time available in civil cases, but since the Courts Act 1988 juries are now only available in defamation cases in the High Court, and in cases involving trespass against the person.

It is unusual for an appellate court to interfere with the quantum of damages awarded but this will be done if the award is grossly disproportionate to the injury suffered. The reluctance to interfere with awards made is particularly acute where the quantum of damages is arrived at by a jury. The appeal court may decide to either substitute a new award or send it back to the trial court to be reassessed on damages.

Where the action is dealt with by the InjuriesBoard.ie the Board will assess the amount of general damages available by reference to their Book of Quantum (see *www.injuriesboard.ie*). Special damages reflecting actual financial loss are also available. Section 22 of the Civil Liability and Courts Act 2004 requires courts to have regard to the Book of Quantum of the InjuriesBoard.ie.

Categories of Damages

A successful plaintiff can be awarded either contemptuous damages, nominal damages, compensatory damages or exemplary damages.

Contemptuous Damages

Contemptuous damages are awarded where a party wins his or her case but the court feels that morally, he or she does not have a right to damages. This may be for instance where the case is technically sound but the plaintiff has acted either harshly or unreasonably in bringing a case. This type of award also has the effect that the court in such a case will not award the plaintiff costs (an exception to the general rule that "costs follow the event.")

Nominal Damages

Nominal damages are awarded where no actual damage has occurred but a right has been infringed. This might occur for instance with the tort of trespass which is *actionable per se*. As described by O'Sullivan J. in *O'Keeffe v Kilcullen*, unreported, High Court, June 24, 1998, "Nominal damages means a sum of money that may be spoken of but has no existence in point of quantity, the purposes of such damages being twofold, namely, either to assert a right or as a 'peg' on which to hang an order for costs."

Compensatory Damages

Compensatory damages are awarded to compensate the victim for the harm done and have traditionally been made up of special damages (pecuniary damages), general damages (non-pecuniary damages) and aggravated damages. Generally speaking general damages are those that are difficult to quantify such as pain, suffering and loss of amenity. Special damages on the other hand are damages of a pecuniary nature such as loss of income and expenses.

Aggravated damages will be awarded to compensate the plaintiff for additional harm suffered as a result of the manner in which the defendant has behaved. In the case of *Conway v Irish National Teachers Organisation* [1991] 2 I.R. 305 Finlay C.J. stated that aggravated damages would be awarded to take into account:

- The manner in which the wrong was committed (did it include oppressiveness, arrogance or outrage),
- The conduct of the wrongdoer after the commission of the wrong, did s/he refuse to apologise, threaten to repeat the wrong?
- The conduct of the defendant or his or her representative in the period coming up to the trial.

In *Cooper v O'Connell*, unreported, Supreme Court, June 5, 1997, a plaintiff unsuccessfully argued for an award of aggravated damages in an action against his dentist for dental work negligently carried out. He argued that he ought to receive aggravated damages due to the fact that the defendant as a medical practitioner had breached a duty of trust, and that he had sought to argue a defence when he had earlier admitted liability. The court disagreed that aggravated damages were appropriate. Finaly C.J. stated that "[an award of] … aggravated damages … must … be in part a recognition of the added hurt or insult to a plaintiff who has been wronged, and in part also a recognition of the cavalier or outrageous conduct of the defendant." The mere fact that he proffered a defence to an action would not in itself amount to a justification for an award of aggravated damages.

More recently, in *Philp v Ryan* [2004] I.E.S.C. 105, a professional negligence action, an award of €50,000 of aggravated damages was made where a doctor had falsified his clinical notes. Generally speaking, an award of aggravated damages is made separately, but Murray C.J. in *Shortt v An Garda Síochána* [2007] I.E.S.C. 9 stated that a global award may be appropriate where the "factors giving rise to aggravated damages are relatively marginal to the substantive wrongs which entitle a plaintiff to ordinary compensatory damages" provided that it is clearly indicated that the award comprises both compensatory and aggravated damages.

Exemplary Damages

Exemplary damages are awarded as a mark of censure of the defendant for the manner in which the tort was committed and as a deterrent to further wrongful behaviour. They are not intended primarily as a means of compensating the victim (unlike aggravated damages) but rather as a means of punishing the defendant. The decision in *Rookes v Barnard* [1964] A.C. 1129 demonstrates the position as regards the awarding of exemplary damages in England. That case laid down three categories where an award of exemplary damages could be made, namely, arbitrary, oppressive or unconstitutional action by the servants of government; wrongdoing calculated to make a profit or statutory cases. It is unclear to what extent the case is applicable in Ireland, as no judgment has yet either completely set aside or conversely completely approved, the decision.

More useful in an Irish context are the guidelines issued by Finlay C.J. in the case of *Conway v Irish National Teachers Organisation* [1991] 2 I.R. 305. In this case the defendants, who were responsible for the plaintiff missing school from August of 1976 until February 1977, were found liable for her loss of education during that time. They appealed an award of £11,500 including £1,500 for exemplary damages. Finlay C.J. did not delimit the categories where exemplary damages would be awarded as had been done in *Rookes*. Rather he stated that one of the possible headings of damages available for breach of a duty in tort was that of:

> "Punitive or exemplary damages arising from the nature of the wrong which was committed and/or the manner of its commission which are intended to mark the court's particular disapproval of the defendant's conduct in all the circumstances of the case and its decision that it should publicly be seen to have punished the defendant for such conduct ..."

In this case as the right infringed was a Constitutional right and the breach was carried out with full knowledge and deliberation, exemplary damages were an appropriate remedy.

Computation of damages

Damages are awarded to make good any loss arising by virtue of physical damage to property and personal injuries. Both categories will include also any economic loss either attaching to such damage or in some cases economic loss standing alone (see Chapter 8). In terms of personal injury, traditionally damages have been divided into two categories, special damages (to compensate pecuniary loss) and general damages (to cover non pecuniary loss).

Physical Damage to Property

Physical damage to land, buildings or other property is measured by reference to its diminution of value as a result of the tort. This will usually consist of the cost incurred to repair the damage or replace the good or in cases where it is irreplaceable an amount reflective of the product or land's market value. In some cases (such as damage to a factory or business) this amount will also include an award for loss of profits or hire costs for replacement products. As discussed in Chapter 2, interest rates on loans required to borrow money to finance any replacement buildings or property will also be compensatable.

Personal injuries

Personal injuries, as stated above, are divided into both special and general damages. Special damages include those damages capable of measurement in monetary terms such as loss of earnings, hospital expenses and other medical expenses. Actuarial evidence is relied on to aid in the assessment of pecuniary loss and awards of damages are tax-free. Any collateral benefits the plaintiff might also recover by virtue of the injury (such as benefits from private insurance, pensions, or any benefit payable under statute or otherwise), will not be deducted from the award of damages made by the court (s.2 Civil Liability (Amendment) Act 1964). Note however that an exception to this general rule applies in the event of disability or injury benefit which is deductible for five years following the date of cause of action (s.75(1) of the Social Welfare (Consolidation) Act 1993).

Loss of Earnings

This includes both loss of earnings up to the time that the negligence arose and future loss of earnings. Calculating future loss of earnings throws up particular difficulties. Such a calculation must take into account issues such as the physical capacity of the plaintiff, the trade or profession of the plaintiff, his or her age and the possibility of retraining. In the case of *Reddy v Bates* [1983] I.R. 141 the Supreme Court stated that the nature of the employment market and the possibility of the plaintiff being unemployed in the future must also be taken into account. In that case the Supreme Court reduced the award of the High Court as its decision had failed to take market conditions into account. In the case of *McMahon v Irish Biscuits Ltd*, unreported, High Court, January 28, 2002, the court made a reduction of 20 per cent to take into account the possibility of the plaintiff being out of work in the future given that he suffered from a bad back. On the other hand, in the case of *O'Neill v Electricity Supply Board*, unreported, High Court, Finnegan P., July 31, 2002 no reduction was made. In that case the plaintiff was a 52 year old employee who had been in uninterrupted employment with the defendants for 34 years and there was no reason to suspect that this would not have continued.

Awards for loss of earnings are made on the basis of the plaintiff's net income, however, if a plaintiff filed inaccurate tax returns or did not declare income for tax purposes the traditional approach has been to exclude such income for assessment of damages purposes (*Glover v BLN (No.2)* [1873] I.R. 432 and s.28(1) of the Civil Liability and Courts Act 2004). An exception to this principle was upheld in *Dowling v O'Flynn* [2000] 4 I.R. 383 where the action was a fatal injuries action taken by the dependents of the deceased (and will most likely survive the Civil Liability and Courts Act 2004 which states in s.28(2) that it does not apply to causes of action accruing prior to the Act and also allows for exceptions in s.28(1) where "the court considers that in all the circumstances it would be unjust to disregard such income, profit or gain".)

Hospital/Carers' Expenses

This includes the cost of all reasonable current or future hospital expenses. It will also include the cost of care in the home should this be required. By virtue of s.75 of the Social Welfare (Consolidation) Act 1993, all statutory disability benefit or injury benefit must be deducted from the amounts calculated. Section 2 of the Health (Amendment) Act 1986 provides that defendants will also have to pay for any hospital or health board costs arising from road accidents. This applies even where the treatment ought otherwise to have been free.

General Damages

These damages include pain and suffering and for generally lesser amounts, loss of expectation of life (also described as loss of amenity). Given the subjective nature of these losses they are notoriously difficult to quantify in monetary terms. In terms of pain and suffering the courts have attempted to develop guidelines for what should be the highest award possible for the most serious injuries by which other awards can then be measured. In the case of *Sinnott v Quinnsworth Ltd* [1984] I.L.R.M. 523 a young man involved in a motor accident was rendered a quadriplegic and left with other physical difficulties which left him entirely dependent on others. He was awarded what was considered the maximum award for such injuries of £150,000. This figure has since increased in line with inflation with an award of £250,000 made in the case of *Kealy v Minister for Health* [1999] 2 I.R. 456 to a woman who had been injected with contaminated Anti-D in 1977. More recently an award of £300,000 was made in the case of *McEneaney v Monaghan County Council*, unreported, High Court, O'Sullivan J., July 26, 2001.

As the damages are to compensate for pain and suffering and loss of expectation in life, a person who responds with optimism to an otherwise debilitating injury might well recover less than a more pessimistic person. Some injuries are also interpreted differently depending on gender. Facial injuries had traditionally been seen to be more traumatic for a woman than a man. The degree to which the "unconscious" patient should be allowed to recover is one which has generated a certain degree of debate. The situation as it stands in Ireland appears to be that an award for general damages will be reduced where the patient is unaware or lacks full awareness of their position, but the reduction will only be moderate, and arises only in the most severe cases (*Cooke v Walsh* [1984] I.L.R.M. 208.)

INJUNCTIONS

Injunctions as an equitable remedy, are awarded where it is "just and convenient" to do so. Injunctions might be sought as a remedy for a number of torts, including those of nuisance, trespass and defamation.

The effect of an injunction can be prohibitory (refraining the defendant from doing something); mandatory (to compel the defendant to undo a wrong or remove a source of risk) or *quia timet* (a pre-emptive injunction to prevent a wrong from occurring in the first place).

The injunction can be granted at the end of the trial period, in which case it is most likely to be a perpetual injunction. An injunction may also be granted as a method of maintaining the status quo until the full trial is heard, in which case the injunction is either an interim injunction or an interlocutory injunction. An interim injunction is an emergency measure, usually granted ex parte before the hearing of the interlocutory proceedings and is only granted where waiting until the interlocutory hearing would result in serious harm. An interlocutory injunction on the other hand will be granted where the following conditions are satisfied: the plaintiff can show that there is a serious question to be tried, the balance of convenience lies in favour of granting an interlocutory injunction and irreparable damage would follow if the injunction were refused.

17. DEFENCES AND LIMITATIONS

INTRODUCTION

In any tort action the claimant must be aware of the defences which exist to defeat a tort action and also to limitation periods which affect the length of time a claimant has to bring a case. In addition to the specific defences discussed under individual torts such as defamation, trespass and the rule in *Rylands v Fletcher*, a number of general defences also exist which are applicable to all torts. These are the defences of contributory negligence (a partial defence), *volenti non fit injuria* (by contract or agreement) and the defence of illegality. In addition to the common law rules, the area of defences is also regulated by the Civil Liability Act 1961.

Limitation periods on the other hand are entirely governed by statute, although there is some room for judicial discretion. Amendments to the limitation periods have recently been introduced by way of the Civil Liability and Courts Act 2004 and with respect to defamation actions, the Defamation Act 2009, and are discussed more fully below.

CONTRIBUTORY NEGLIGENCE

Prior to the introduction of the Civil Liability Act 1961 the existence of contributory negligence acted as a complete defence for a defendant. This rule was particularly harsh and the court attempted to avoid it where possible. As a result the rule of "last clear chance" was devised which provided that if the defendant had the last opportunity to avoid the accident and failed to do so by his negligence then the action could still run. The law was clearly in need of reform and this was achieved in 1961. The present law in this area is that where a plaintiff has contributed to his injury damages will be reduced in proportion to his or her fault (s.34(1) Civil Liability Act 1961). In addition, where a plaintiff has failed to mitigate his/her damages this will also be deemed to be contributory negligence and the court will reduce the award accordingly (s.34(2) Civil Liability Act 1961).

Basis for Contributory Negligence

In order for a plaintiff to be liable for contributory negligence the defendant must show that the plaintiff behaved unreasonably given the circumstances. What is reasonable is addressed in the same way as reasonableness in negligence cases generally with some leniency provided for those with limited capacity. It will not, for instance, amount to contributory negligence not to look down when walking (*Sheehy v The Devil's Glen Tours Equestrian Centre Ltd*, unreported, High Court, Lavan J., December 2001). Nor will it necessarily amount to contributory negligence to continuing a poor work practice if this practice is one which is common and has gone uncorrected at the place of work (*Stewart v Killeen Paper Mills Ltd* [1959] I.R. 436). In the case of those who become voluntarily intoxicated the standard applied is that of a sober plaintiff. In the case of *Boyne v Bus Átha Cliath*, unreported, High Court, Finnegan P., April, 2002, Finnegan P. made it clear that the plaintiff who was intoxicated at the time he stumbled in front of the bus would be assessed for contributory negligence as if he were sober. In this case contributory negligence of 25 per cent was found.

Apportionment

Section 34(1) of the Civil Liability Act provides that where the damage suffered by the plaintiff results partly from the defendant's wrong and partly from the plaintiff's own negligence (or the negligence of someone for whom the plaintiff is responsible) then the damages awarded may be apportioned between them.

Damages are apportioned "as the court thinks just and equitable" based on the degree of fault of each party. Section 31(1)(a) states that where it is not possible to establish degrees of fault, liability will be apportioned equally.

Fault

Section 34(1)(a) requires an apportionment of damages to be made according to degrees of fault. Fault has been described in a number of cases as equating to "blameworthiness" rather than to the extent that each party had caused the accident. In the case of *O'Sullivan v Dwyer* [1971] I.R. 275, Walsh J., held that "fault" equated with moral blameworthiness, measured against the degree of capacity or knowledge which such person ought to have had if he were an ordinary, reasonable person.

Kenny J. in *Carroll v Clare County Council* [1975] I.R. 221 also referred to the distinction between causation and fault, stating that the question was not to what extent both parties caused the accident but as to how "blameworthy" both parties were. In that case the plaintiff, tired after a long day and having consumed between four and six beers, had an accident when completing a junction. Although the County Council were found negligent in their road maintenance, the plaintiff was also found 30 per cent contributory negligence.

Duty to Mitigate Damages

Section 34(2)(b) of the Civil Liability Act 1961 states that a negligent or careless failure to mitigate damage is deemed to be contributory negligence in respect of the amount by which such damage exceeds the damage that would otherwise have occurred. So for instance if a plaintiff fails to undergo medical treatment, or fails to take reasonable steps to secure employment or fails to make use of any protective equipment, this may amount to contributory negligence. In the case of *Bohan v Finn* D.P.I.J.: Trinity and Michaelmas Terms 1994, for instance, the failure of a plaintiff suffering from psychosomatic illness to undergo treatment in a psychiatric unit which carried a very high chance of a cure, was held to amount to contributory negligence. Similarly, failure to wear a seat beat when this increases the injury suffered will result in a reduction in the award of damages. As stated in *Hamill v Oliver* [1977] I.R. 73:

> "Any person who travels in the front seat of a motor car, be he passenger or driver, without wearing an available seat belt must normally be held guilty of contributory negligence if the injuries in respect of which he sues were caused wholly or in part as a result of his failure to wear a seat belt."

VOLENTI NON FIT INJURIA

In its early form any form of voluntary assumption of risk was fatal to the plaintiff's case. This position has been altered by s.34(1)(b) of the Civil Liability Act 1961 which states that in cases that might otherwise have attracted the defence of voluntary assumption of risk, the defence of contributory negligence will apply instead. In other words behaviour which would at one time constitute a voluntary assumption of the risk of injury will now be classed as contributory negligence only and the action will stand. Two exceptions to this general rule exist: where a contract exists which amounts to a clear undertaking of the risk or where the complainant has agreed to waive his legal rights to an action.

Contract

If a contractual provision exists between both parties where the claimant clearly states that they are willing to adopt the risk associated with the activity the claimant will be deemed to have assumed the risk involved and will lose their right to sue (s.34(1)(b)). Such contracts are however strictly construed and the courts do not look too favourably on such contracts. For such a contract to be effective it would need to be clearly drafted and communicated prior to any exclusion being effective. As stated by Walsh J. in *O'Hanlon v ESB* [1969] I.R. 75:

> "It is already settled that such contracts are construed strictly against the party claiming the benefit of the exception and there are instances where such contracts are actually prohibited by statute."

Agreement to Waive Rights

A clear agreement by the plaintiff to waive his rights in relation to any potential action will also defeat a claim. However, as with the exception provided for contracts, this exception is narrowly interpreted. The agreement must have involved some communication between the parties so that it could reasonably be inferred that the plaintiff had waived his legal rights. If this is not present undertaking the risk will amount at most to contributory negligence by the plaintiff.

The issue of whether a legitimate waiver existed arose in the case of *McComiskey v McDermott* [1974] I.R. 75. In this case the plaintiff was the navigator in a rally and was travelling in a car driven by the defendant. On the dashboard of the car there was a notice which stated that passengers travelled at their own risk. Following an accident the defendant sought to rely on the notice as a waiver of the plaintiff's right to sue. The court applied *O'Hanlon v ESB* and held that there had been no communication between the parties on the issue of a waiver and in these circumstances the defence was not applicable. Griffin J. did however state that: "In an appropriate case the affixing of a notice to the dashboard might lead to the inference that there was agreement between the passenger and the owner sufficient to set up the statutory defence ..."

As regards rescuers who go to the aid of someone in danger they are generally not seen to have waived their right to bring an action. Similarly, in the case of employees such as the police, army officers or others who engage in activities involving risk, their right of action remains despite an apparent acceptance of the risk involved.

ILLEGALITY

The defence of illegality reflects the common law principle of ex turpi causa non oritur action, which means that a person cannot seek a remedy under an illegal transaction in which they have participated. However, s.57(1) of the Civil Liability Act 1961 makes it clear that simply showing that the plaintiff is in breach of the civil or criminal law will not bar an action. This in effect makes this common law principle largely redundant today for the purpose of the Irish courts.

LIMITATION PERIODS

A claimant has a limited amount of time in which to bring an action after which the statute of limitations is said to run out and they can no longer seek a remedy. Limitation periods are determined by statute and are governed for the purposes of tort actions by the Statute of Limitations Act 1957, the Statute of Limitations (Amendment) Acts 1991 and 2000, the Civil Liability Act 1961 and more recently the Civil Liability and Courts Act 2004.

The general rule is provided in s.11 of the Statute of Limitations Act 1957, which states that tort actions shall not be brought more than 6 years after the date on which the cause of action accrued. This would include damage to property, trespass actions and economic loss actions. Section 38(1) of the Defamation Act 2009 amends this section in relation to defamation actions by reducing the limitation period from six years to one year, or "such longer period as the court may direct" but not exceeding two years.

For personal injuries actions caused by negligence, nuisance or breach of duty (contract, statutory or otherwise) the limitation period is two years from the date of accrual of the cause of action (reduced from three years by s.7 of the Civil Liability and Courts Act 2004 amending s.11 Statute of Limitations (Amendment) Act 1991). The "date of accrual" is central to any action and arises either on the date the wrongful act occurred (for torts which are actionable per se), or on the date on which damage arose (for those torts not actionable per se). For torts which are continuous (such as nuisance) the date is the date of the last instance of the tort.

While the date on which most tort actions can be taken runs from the date of accrual, for personal injuries cases the limitation period is more flexible, running either from the date on which the cause of action accrued, or the "date of knowledge" whichever is later. This is to allow a plaintiff time to become aware of any injury they might have and time to determine its cause. The "date of knowledge" is defined in s.2(1) of the 1991 Act as being the date on which the plaintiff has knowledge of the following facts:

• that the person alleged to have been injured has been injured;
• that the injury in question was significant;
• that the injury was connected to the act of the defendant;
• the identity of the defendant;
• the identity of a third party who caused the injury, and the basis of a claim against the defendant.

Extended/reduced Periods

An extended period is provided to those who are said to be "under a disability". In such a case time does not begin to run until after the plaintiff ceases to be under a disability.

"Disability" is defined in s.48(1) of Statute of Limitations Act 1957 as including:

• An infant (under the age of 21).
• A person of unsound mind.
• A convict subject to the operation of the Forfeiture Act, 1870, in whose case no administrator or curator has been appointed under that Act.
• A victim of sexual abuse who is suffering from consequent psychological injury.

This last provision relating to victims of abuse was inserted into the 1957 Act by s.2 of the Statute of Limitations (Amendment) Act 2000.

The Liability of Defective Products Acts 1991 also imposes a limitation period of three years after the date of damage or "knowledge" and 10 years after the product was put into circulation, regardless of discovery.

Reduced limitation periods apply in two cases. The first applies to injury or damage caused by a sea vessel to another vessel or to persons or property on board a vessel, in which case the limitation period is two years (s.46(2) of the Civil Liability Act 1961). This period however, can be extended by the court if such an extension is reasonable. The second applies in actions taken against the estate of a person who is deceased. Such actions may be taken if existing at the time of the respondent's death, or otherwise within two years of the respondent's death (s.9(2) of the Civil Liability Act 1961). This provision does not apply to cases taken under the Liability for Defective Products Act 1991.

FURTHER REFORM

The most recent reform of this area has been brought about by the Civil Liability and Courts Act 2004. The Act was signed into law on July 21, 2004, the majority of sections however were not commenced until September 2004 with final sections commencing in March 2005 (Civil Liability and Courts Act 2004 (Commencement) Order 2004). The most significant amendment brought about by the Act is the reduction of the limitation period for personal injuries actions to two years from the date of accrual of the cause of action or the date of knowledge of the cause of action whichever occurs later (discussed above). The Act also requires (since September 2004) that the claimant issues a notice to the respondent within two months of the date of the cause of action outlining details as to the claim in question (s.8 of the 2004 Act). Failure to do so without reasonable cause will allow the court, where justice requires, to "draw inferences" from such a failure or to deny or reduce the costs that might otherwise be payable to the plaintiff. The other significant provisions are s.25 and s.26 (commenced in September 2004). Section 25 makes it an offence for anyone to knowingly give false or misleading evidence in a personal injuries action to a solicitor or an expert, with the intention of misleading the court. Section 26 provides that where a plaintiff gives false or misleading evidence with the intention of misleading the court then the court will dismiss the plaintiff's action entirely, unless the plaintiff can show that this would result in an "injustice" being done. The penalty for an offence under the Act is significant. The guilty party can be made liable, upon conviction on indictment, to a maximum fine of €100,000, or imprisonment for a term of up to 10 years, or to both. If tried summarily the person guilty of the offence can be liable for a fine not exceeding €3,000, or imprisonment for a term not exceeding 12 months, or to both. In tandem with the establishment of the Personal Injuries Assessment Board (now InjuriesBoard.ie) these measures are intended to significantly reduce the number of costly and/or fraudulent claims before the courts.

INDEX

147